Priests in a
People's Church

A sequel to
The Fire and the Clay

In memory of Christopher Gray

Priests in a People's Church

Peter Allan CR
Sister Barbara June SLG
Benjamin Gordon-Taylor
John Gribben CR
George Guiver CR
Christine Henshall
Nicholas Henshall
Charles Pickstone
Margaret Selby

Published in Great Britain in 2001 by
Society for Promoting Christian Knowledge
Holy Trinity Church
Marylebone Road
London NW1 4DU

British Library Cataloguing-in-Publication Data

A catalogue record for this book is available from the British Library

ISBN 0-281-05405-3

Typeset by Krystyna Hewitt, Chinnor, Oxfordshire
Printed in Great Britain by
Antony Rowe Ltd, Chippenham, Wiltshire

Contents

Acknowledgements   vi

The authors   vi

Introduction   vii

PART ONE: PERCEPTIONS

1   The Priest and the Mystery: A Case of Identity   3

2   Screen Idol   25

3   The Priest in the Media Age   33

4   A Word from One of the *Laos*   51

PART TWO: THE PRIEST IN RELATIONSHIP

5   Simple Gifts: Priesthood in a Praying Community   63

6   Priest and Victim   73

7   Marriage, Priesthood and Ministry: Four Vignettes   85

8   The Priest, Sex and Society   101

9   Detachment in Priesthood and Community   115

10   The Priest as Focus   127

Notes   139

Index   145

Acknowledgements

The authors are particularly grateful to Jonathan Greener, Thomas Seville CR and David Wylie for their contribution to the genesis of this book.

The authors

Peter Allan CR, Director of Studies, College of the Resurrection, Mirfield

Sister Barbara June SLG, Community of the Sisters of the Love of God, Fairacres

Benjamin Gordon-Taylor, Solway Fellow and Chaplain, University College, Durham

John Gribben CR, Former Tutor and Registrar, College of the Resurrection, Mirfield

George Guiver CR, Vice-Principal, College of the Resurrection, Mirfield

Christine Henshall, Journalist

Nicholas Henshall, Vicar of St Margaret's, Scotswood, Newcastle

Charles Pickstone, Vicar of St Laurence's, Catford, London

Margaret Selby, Former Director of Pastoral Studies, College of the Resurrection, Mirfield

Introduction

Wombat – Australian herbivorous marsupial
mammal esp. of genus *Phascolomis*, like a small bear.
(Concise Oxford Dictionary)

In asking the question, 'What is a priest?' we meet a problem: it is impossible to talk about priesthood in isolation. We can ask, What is a wombat or an edible dormouse?, but not, What is a priest? The priest is no independent species – the 'laity' are part of the picture of what the priest is, and the priest is part of the picture of what the laity are. We can see the oddity of it by comparing with ballroom dancing: you can't sit down and discuss what a partner is. 'These are the characteristics of a partner,' we would be saying, 'and so-and-so has been called to be a dancing-partner, and will go to dancing school to pursue individual research on what it is to be a partner.' To understand the word 'partner' you need to dance with your partners, and any theorizing will be about dancing. There are limitations to putting the notion 'priest' under the microscope – in the life of the gospel it is like 'partner' in dancing.

A contemporary understanding of priesthood within the Church can only be discovered in the context of the whole people of God. Today we find it difficult to see what in the priestly role distinguishes it from any other kind of leadership. Many reduce it to simply that – the priest as the leader and chief administrator/co-ordinator of the Christian community. We are uncomfortable with nostalgia and fantasy about superhuman figures, wizards or fairy godmothers, and so shy away from seeing the priest in transcendental terms. Our problem lies partly in the framing of our questions in the first place. Almost any terminology appears beset with problems: even the title of this book, which frequently gains an enthusiastic response. The phrase 'a people's Church' might catch our imagination, but has a powerful shadow side. Recent political history painfully demonstrates how a self-proclaimed 'people's' society can be at least as short-sighted and tyrannical as a hierarchical one. Many of us have a great desire for a Church of the people, but there is less care in asking questions about what we presuppose by this, and some would say there is not enough care today in ensuring we are *God's* Church. 'Priests in God's Church' would not have been half as appealing as a title, and that reflects something about presuppositions. 'Priests in' is a problem as well, implying the introduction of something distinct into an already-existing church body. We have to ask questions too about the word 'priest' in an age that recognizes a priesthood in all baptized Christians.

Across the worldwide Church, in most of the mainstream denominations in fact, there is uncertainty and disorientation about the nature of ordained Christian ministry. Newly-ordained clergy in the Church of England belong to post-ordination training groups during their first years, and there they discover often with some shock that the diversity they knew in their training is nothing like the diversity of views and practice they now find out in the field. The groups can include people with a fairly traditional, high view of priesthood in the catholic mould, and others eager to insist they are no different from anybody else. If we think that is a problem of the Church of England with its tradition of wide diversity, then we only need to cross the road to discover this situation in the other churches too. I recently heard a complaint from young catholic priest in Italy that his young priests' group poured scorn on the saying of the daily office, and were riddled with uncertainty as to what their role today is as priests. If we were to look at the Lutherans in Germany or Sweden, or come back across the waters to look at British Methodism, we would find the same.

There is no need to repeat here all of the factors underlying this uncertainty, from the expansion of lay ministry to the loss of a sense of God's transcendence. They are repeatedly cited as indications of a crisis. It is tempting in response to disorientation to look for a satisfying model, but we should beware of quests for the Holy Grail. In this book we offer no model which will tidy all the problems up. On the other hand, we do believe in something, and that belief motivates us to write. We hope this will become clear from what we have written, not as a monolithic answer to all the questions, but an intertwining of related views about a shared conviction: a dialogue, a dance, if you like, around a question to which there is no simple answer, and yet about which there are some definite things to be said that can help us make sense of our disorientation. Similarly, having said the title of our book bristles with questions, we have nevertheless chosen this title because we like it – it catches an intuition of the age, and proclaims a truth: ordained priesthood cannot be understood, nor even sensibly discussed, except in terms of the relationship between priests, people and God.

Our exploration does not attempt to cover all the ground: we trace a particular pathway, taking present-day perceptions of the priestly office as our launch pad, starting appropriately with mystery, a word that discourages definitive statements but is the opposite of reductionism. Lightness of touch and dancing feet are the only way to court this particular truth: it will not fit into neat boxes, and asks us to hold together surprising contrasts. An unusual analogue is then found in the screen idol: a public figure who gathers up intuitions and truths about ourselves and mirrors them back to us in a way with which we can identify. This leads naturally into the media, and the contemporary perceptions and stereotypes that they draw on, the conclusion being that here is a source of reflection on priesthood that we need to take seriously. Then Margaret Selby boldly paints in one or two of those things that the people of God fervently desire to see in their priests and don't find often enough. A picture of priesthood for today can only be found if the *laos*, the company of the baptized, can play a full part in the search, and this chapter sets down an important marker.

Next we select some facets of the question which seem to us to be important, and which were not fully taken up in our previous volume, *The Fire and the Clay*. We believe the monastic tradition offers a wealth of riches to contemporary Christians, and make no apology for offering insights from the life of a convent. Life in community naturally leads on to a chapter which examines the priest's calling to look beyond outward appearance to what is going on in the person within. Marriage, the single life and sexuality demand careful reflection today, and we try to offer in the next two chapters a contribution to the debate. After four chapters on the closeness of human relating comes a counterweight: the lonely position of the priest is both darkness and light, and we need to remember it includes the need for detachment. This isolation in the midst of many people brings us back to the paradox with which we began: the priest among the priestly people stands at a focal point where many lines converge.

As in *The Fire and the Clay*, the authors represent a diversity of views, not least on the ordination of women, and we particularly want to offer this witness to the possibility of working wholeheartedly together with respect for each other's views, a close working which here has produced no mere collection of essays, but a fruit of common effort over a long period.

Priests in a People's Church is intended as a sequel to *The Fire and the Clay*, which was written in response to a particular situation: the proposal to close the College of the Resurrection, Mirfield. We were clear when we had finished that book that there was more to be said, and there would need to be a sequel. Having done this, we are now even more aware that the mystery deepens and attracts still further. In the meantime the group has lost some authors and gained others. We particularly mourn the loss of Christopher Gray, murdered in the course of his pastoral duties. That tremendous loss to the Church on earth is not, we are sure, seen as such by the Church in Heaven, and it is to his memory, and in response to his present prayers for us, that we dedicate this book.

GEORGE GUIVER

PART ONE
PERCEPTIONS

1

The Priest and the Mystery:
A Case of Identity

BENJAMIN GORDON-TAYLOR

> When Jesus came to the region of Caesarea Philippi he put this
> question to his disciples, 'Who do people say the Son of
> Man is?' And they said, 'Some say he is John the Baptist, some
> Elijah, and others Jeremiah or one of the prophets'. 'But you,'
> he said 'who do you say I am?'
> (Matt. 16.13–14, *Jerusalem Bible*)

In his book *Lake Wobegon Days*, Garrison Keillor describes a priest who
has been covering for a colleague who is on holiday. Father Frank, the
substitute, is very different from Father Emil, the parish priest, and he
challenges parishioners' ideas about what a priest should be like:

> With Father's return imminent, the parish bade farewell to his
> sub, Father Frank. The Kruegers threw a cocktail party for
> him in their backyard where they have a concrete patio and a
> glass-top table with umbrella (green-striped) attached. The
> guest list was small; not many Catholics in town are comfort-
> able around a priest in a sportshirt and yellow shorts, drink-
> ing gin and saying, '*Damn*, this is good, Jack. *Dry*.
> Mmmmmm. What did you do? Just *think* about vermouth, for
> Christ's sake?'[1]

Father Frank doesn't measure up to the expectations of many Catholics in
Lake Wobegon because his appearance and manner do not fit with their
acquired criteria of priestly behaviour. They assess him according to what
they see and hear, and effectively reject him. He does not fit the pattern
to which they have become used. For them, his identity as a priest is
called into question by yellow shorts, gin and colourful language. While
this raises important questions for clergy about conformity to cultural
conventions, it also draws attention to the deeper theological question of
priestly identity. Who do people say a priest is? In what way does the priest
relate to the mystery of God in Christ, the paschal mystery, which the
whole Church celebrates and makes present? What is it about a priest
that gives this identity and animates it for the whole people of God? A

renewed appreciation of mystery can help to answer these questions, and indeed encourage us to ask them in the first place. It can also help to reinterpret ordained priesthood in the context of the ministry of all the baptized, and perhaps bring new life to the practice of a ministry which some would see as increasingly inappropriate or irrelevant.

Priests in a people's church

A rediscovery of mystery in connection with priesthood needs to be seen in the context of the changing theological relationship between baptism and ordination, and the questioning of 'priesthood' itself. In the Western Church, the Second Vatican Council's Constitution on the Church, *Lumen Gentium*, signified a radical reappraisal and renewal of the theology of the Church which has had an impact beyond the Roman Catholic Church.[2] No longer is it possible to talk of a 'top down' Church, with clearly defined layers of ministry and authority and an inherited distancing of ordained ministers and lay people, although the present papacy has perhaps at least slowed down the trend away from this under-standing. By and large, the last 30 years have seen not so much a narrowing of the gap between priests and lay people as a wholesale reorientation of the terms in which these categories are understood. It has been the emergence of a strong theology of baptism that has exposed the need for an equally penetrating theology of ordination. It is an acknowledged matter of regret that Vatican II really failed to provide this:

> The presbyterate suffered from the poor emphasis it received in *Lumen Gentium*. It was a pity that it was not treated with more depth and in greater unity with episcopate, and that in fact the whole ordained ministry was not treated more comprehensively.[3]

This failure to provide an adequate theology of priesthood was echoed to some degree at an institutional level in other communions that retain the threefold ordained ministry of bishop, priest and deacon. Nevertheless, the period since the Council has seen much discussion of particular issues, and the writing of a great many helpful and penetrating studies of the theological and pastoral dimensions of priesthood and ministry.

The priesthood was once seen as having a particular ethos and spirituality almost totally distinct from that of lay people in the parish and essentially separate from their experience of daily life. Priests were officially encouraged to be the spiritual and ministerial élite, with effective absolute control over all aspects of parish life, although in Anglican parishes this authority has always been tempered by the existence of elected lay officers. In general, lay people tended to be liturgical spectators and the *recipients* of teaching and pastoral care, with little opportunity for being *participants* in all these areas of ministry. Ordination (or sometimes the monastic life) was considered to be the sole route to active ministry. There was little or no sense of baptism being any more than an impoverished badge of membership, the mere passport to *reception* of the other sacraments, instead of a disclosure of the paschal mystery which enabled *participation* in them and which held the possibility of active lay ministry in the Church. Ministry was something done by priests and received by lay people, and there was little concept of shared mission. The consequences of this are sadly still obvious in a great many Anglican parishes, and not necessarily in those which have become labelled 'traditionalist'. Reports and recent discussion in Roman Catholic journals suggest that there exist similar tensions in that Church even three decades after Vatican II – parish priests are not obliged to have parish councils, and indeed may disband an existing one.

In spite of this, the significance of Vatican II for all the Western Churches cannot be underestimated. The Council signalled a return to the biblical and patristic roots of all aspects of the Church, and created the potential for fundamental structural change and spiritual renewal. The personalities, pastoral priorities and spiritual depth of Popes John XXIII and Paul VI were critical in this and, in spite of curial opposition, enabled there to be a sensible reassessment of previous certainties and a corresponding real experience of renewal in the parish life of many priests and people, which spilled over into the Anglican communion and other churches. A Roman Catholic priest has written movingly of the effects at parish level, making possible

> a prayer life that was not separated from daily life but flowed from it and into it. It was experienced and enriched in every aspect of our daily ministry and was not experienced apart from the laity, but shared with them, because this was a spirituality flowing from baptism and not from ordination.[4]

The implications of this experience for the ordained ministry in all traditions are enormous. The practical rediscovery of the baptismal ministry of the whole people of God in the period since Vatican II has underlined the healthy need for the traditional forms of ordained ministry within it to be further explored and set in context, but without shying away from the challenges that have inevitably arisen.

Even before the Council, there were signs of the radical shift to come that began to formulate the questions that would need to be asked about the relationship between priest and baptized lay person. The Liturgical Movement was one such precursor in both its Roman Catholic and

Anglican forms. J. D. Crichton has shown in a recent study that the roots of the need for renewal at the heart of the Church's life as a worshipping community can be traced back a remarkably long way.[5] Other voices included that of Thomas Merton, who in the 1950s predicted the agenda that would emerge after the Council by asking:

> What is the function of the priest in the world? To teach other men? To advise them? To console them? To pray for them? These things enter into his life, but they can be done by anyone ... These actions require no special priesthood, other than our baptismal participation in the priesthood of Christ, and they can be exercised even without this.[6]

His remarks are all the more significant in that he was himself ordained in a monastic setting completely apart from the parish ministry of priests. Furthermore, questions of this kind did not arise only in Roman Catholic circles. In the immediate wake of the Council and before its significance was fully known the Anglican theologian Austin Farrer, in a classic sermon on priesthood, challenged his hearers that

> There is nothing to stop a layman from being a more learned and a more penetrating theologian than the priest of his parish; nothing, certainly to prevent a layman from being a much more understanding helper of people in any sort of trouble or sorrow. What distinctive place does [the priest] hold in the mighty purpose of God?[7]

Despite marked differences of setting and period, Merton and Farrer ask essentially the same questions: What is it about the priest that is distinctive? How is the priest to be identified?

Crisis and controversy

In the 30 and more years since the Council, the uneven renewal of parish life has not caused this question to go away. Indeed it has to be seen also against the less encouraging backdrop of what many recognize to be a crisis in ordained ministry. This crisis has made itself known most obviously in the Roman Catholic Church, in which the period has seen a steep decline in the number of active priests, the result of fewer offering themselves for ordination and a large number of departures from active ministry.[8] In many parts of the Anglican Communion there has also been a decline in active numbers and a similar shortage of candidates. There is an increased questioning of the very necessity for a ministerial priesthood, finding expression in the Anglican communion in the debate about lay presidency at the Eucharist. There are also ongoing debates about ministry in both the Roman and Anglican Communions on issues presented by their supporters as potential enrichments of the priesthood, which are held to address theological questions as to who may be a priest, and some of the practical problems of decreasing numbers. Examples of these debates are the ordination of married men and the ordination of women. All these factors suggest that there is within Anglicanism and increasingly in the Roman Catholic Church (in spite of statements from the Vatican) a crisis of confidence in and a diversity of understanding of priesthood that threatens to destabilize its unifying character and make it impossible to have much shared sense of its identity.

A more urgent task?
Some would therefore see specific issues as secondary, and the urgency of debate lying in another direction. Michael Richards has argued that

> The crisis of conscience experienced by many Anglican clergy over the ordination of women has brought out still further the need for a clarification of the character of the ministry in question. On this point above all depend the further questions of who should receive ordination and by whom it must legitimately be conferred.[9]

This has been echoed by other recent writers, notably Alwyn Marriage in her challenging study, *The People of God: A Royal Priesthood*:

> The controversies and disagreements of the Church over the eligibility of certain groups of people to be ordained has ensured that the term 'priest' has had its fair share of media attention ... This, however, has only served to allow Christians to avoid the central issue of what priesthood actually is.[10]

Wherever one stands in whatever debate, responses to the question 'Who *may be* a priest?' do not in themselves answer the underlying, primary question, 'Who or what *is* a priest?', but tend to address single issues in what can be a negative context of vociferous controversy. Added to this is the number of categories of ordained ministry now existing in the Church of England that are superimposed on the historic priesthood – if to be seen as authentic expressions of it, these surely need a convinced theology of ordination to underpin them. An urgent task would therefore seem to be to seek a more positive and primary rediscovery and restatement of the meaning of ordination in terms that avoid clericalism (an entirely different thing) and affirm the baptismal context of all ministry. This is an essential task if priesthood is to be taken at all seriously and celebrated as something theologically legitimate and indispensable in the understanding and life of the Church past, present and to come. Specific issues, though important, have tended to be disproportionate in their influence. They are part of the discussion and evolution of forms of ministry, whether in a positive or a negative sense, but will be addressed with confidence by those minded to support and oppose them only if the universal foundations are first explored and celebrated. This is where mystery can help.

Mystery and Scripture

Scripture is at the heart of the life of the Church, animating our relationship with God as a means through which Christ is formed in us. It can be described as the 'living' word because it is ultimately rooted in the infinite mystery of the living God. It is not simply a lifeless text or a set of instructions, but an objective engagement with God which is not defined by fundamental literalism, by a historical approach devoid of theological reflection, or by a particular critical method or school.

St Augustine was astonished to see St Ambrose reading silently to himself instead of following the usual custom of reading aloud, which

> was not only considered normal; it was considered necessary for the full comprehension of a text. Augustine believed that reading needed to be present; that within the confines of a page the *scripta*, the written words, had to become *verba*, spoken words, in order to spring into being. For Augustine, the reader had to breathe life into a text, to fill the created space with living language.[11]

Scripture lives as the agent of the mystery, not the master, and the 'created space' between the text and ourselves is filled by the living God who breathes life into us. To the believer, Scripture is not primarily a historical source, but a part of God's self-communication with us. For the people of God, it is a disclosure of the infinite mystery of God that enables us to participate in that mystery, and does not depend on the historian's emphasis on evidence for its true purpose. After all, those who seek in biblical texts a conclusive, clear-cut presentation of the origins, development and theological identity of the Christian ordained ministry will be disappointed. Although the interpretation of the historical and theological evidence is an important task, it is not an end in itself. There is a tension between biblical scholarship and the use of the Bible in the life of the

Church and the individual Christian that must be acknowledged as much in a discussion of ministry as in any other area.

An essay in the book *Europe without Priests?* admits the difficulty of trying to relate the forms of ministry which exist today to the textual evidence of the New Testament and its presentation of Jesus:

> The identification of the Twelve with apostles and the succession to them in the later *episkopoi* clearly does not go back to the explicit will of the historical or risen Lord. There is no indication whatsoever that Jesus himself ever thought in terms of *episkopoi*, presbyters or deacons. [12]

This is not at all to deny that the apostolic mission and developed ordained ministry of the Church are a direct result of the mission of the Twelve, a mission given them by Jesus, and a legitimate expression of his will in the context of that mission, but shaped by the emerging and developing tradition of the Church under the guidance of the Holy Spirit. And yet, historical or theological justification within the text of scripture for Christian priesthood as we have received it is largely *implicit* rather than *explicit*, and it has developed within wider terms of reference than what can be gleaned solely from the text of the New Testament. This does not have to make it unacceptable or somehow not of God (although admittedly it does for some Christians), but it ought to lead us to ask what legitimate relationship it has to the mystery of God of which it is also the servant, to which scripture and the tradition of the Church witness, and which is revealed in the person of Jesus Christ as we see him through the lens of the Gospels *and* experience him now in life, liturgy and prayer. An approach that acknowledges mystery frees us from looking only for evidence of ministry being exercised or for signs of 'intent', and drawing from them largely academic conclusions. This is not only an academic matter, but is also to do with the spiritual journey of the whole Church with and into God, and its experience of Father, Son and Holy Spirit present and active in the world throughout all ages. Henri de Lubac reminds us of St Bernard's warning to those who are content to be mere theological 'investigators':

> we shall find him as severe as the Cappadocians or John Chrysostom on the rashness which makes a man an 'investigator' or 'raider on Majesty'; like the Book of Proverbs, he predicts that such a man will be 'crushed by the Glory'; no doubt, he explains, it is possible to approach it, but 'as one marvelling, not as one investigating', and this presupposes that the initiative comes from God. [13]

The context of priesthood, as of all life and all ministry, is the mystery of God encountered in the living word, dwelling in the Church, and shown forth in our lives.

The language of mystery

Applying the language of mystery to priesthood may seem to sit uncomfortably with the fact that the priest has in a certain sense been 'de-mystified' by the rediscovery of baptism. Certain liturgical and pastoral ministries previously carried out only by priests are now rightly seen to be within the capability of all the baptized, and should be equally or more properly theirs. These ministries are therefore much less 'mysterious', because they have quite rightly become once more the pos- session of the whole people of God. There has been a healthy need to explain and justify their purpose, but not a lessening of their importance. The same is also true of the tasks that continue to be part of the priest's ministry, and of the nature of ordained priesthood. It is actually exercised by those called and authorized to do so, but like all ministry, is the possession of the whole Church and therefore open to enquiry and explo- ration by those who do not exercise it as well as by those who do. If this is so, to speak in terms of mystery can seem to imply a lack of confidence or certainty, or indeed an excuse for continuing traditional forms for no good reason.

But asking how mystery can have this role is also to accept the challenge of trying to talk about something which, because it is of God, is ultimately inexpressible:

> Mystery is the ground throughout, yet withdraws all the more; it is the foundation throughout but does not come under our control … we can speak in reaction to it but never really about it.[14]

To acknowledge our limited mental engagement with mystery is to accept 'God's incomprehensibility as God'.[15] Crucially, it is also to realize the infinite possibility of encounter with God. Rudolf Otto described the mys- tery of God as both daunting and fascinating: recognition of its enormity is accompanied by an irresistible urge to be drawn into its depths, to be shown wonders, to marvel.[16] Something of this urge to probe the unknown is shown in Roald Dahl's dark tale, ostensibly for children, *Charlie and the Chocolate Factory*, in which the irresistible mystery of Willy Wonka's sweet factory sends the world into a frenzy when an opportunity is given to find a 'golden ticket' and pass beyond the locked gates to wonders that have hitherto only been imagined, and only made tangible in the form of chocolate bars. We are drawn to the hidden depths of God, knowing only too well that for us there is no 'golden ticket', much less a glass elevator, and yet the desire for God is there.

Mystery is therefore not a convenient theological smokescreen or ecclesiological cop-out, but an expression of the infinite potential of our engagement with God and his with us, most perfectly expressed in the Word made flesh, Jesus Christ. Mystery is not a lifeless theoretical principle: it exists in relation to us, we engage with it, find it within ourselves, and are changed by it. God's self-communication in mystery draws us in and feeds our fascination with him – God moves towards us, and we are enabled to move towards him. In exploring the meaning of priesthood, then, we must allow God to take the initiative. We must allow God to show us how the mystery is disclosed in scripture, in the Church, in priesthood, and in us.

Mystery and sacrament

The twentieth century saw a rediscovery of mystery as a dynamic theological concept and as a component in a renewed sacramental theology. Several pioneering voices have reminded the Church of its patristic and linguistic context, among them Dom Odo Casel, the German Benedictine who formulated a wide-ranging 'mystery-theology' in the 1930s and 1940s. Most importantly, we have been recalled to the fact that 'mystery' and 'sacrament' have the same origin as theological terms, being Greek and Latin equivalents: *mysterion* and *sacramentum*. Generally speaking, in the Western Church 'sacrament' has since the Middle Ages been understood in a relatively narrow way, as a word describing a limited number of fixed channels through which grace is dispensed, as if the God who meets us in the sacraments is somehow constrained in his power to communicate himself to us, and almost suggesting that we can control him in this way. In the West, 'mystery' has been reserved mainly for the incomprehensibility of God in a theoretical sense. In the Christian East, however, 'mystery' retained a much more dynamic understanding, and is used in the context of the sacraments as manifestations of the mystery of God in its fullness and vitality. In the West, we are rediscovering this dynamic understanding, and realizing once more that God enters into a *living* relationship with us through the sacraments, or *mysteries*, themselves disclosures of the one mystery of God in Christ.

The presence of Christ in his mysteries

This leads us to appreciate a broader view of the nature of Christ's presence in the liturgy than traditional Western theology has tended to admit. We can now talk of '*Presence*, seen as a *mystery* with many aspects, and not simply as a *miracle*'.[17] It is partly this insight which lies behind the Vatican II Constitution on the Liturgy in saying:

> Christ is always present in his Church, especially in her liturgical celebrations. He is present in the sacrifice of the Mass, not only in the person of his minister ... but especially under the eucharistic species. By his power he is present in the sacraments, so that when anybody baptizes it is really Christ himself who baptizes. He is present in his word, since it is he himself who speaks when the holy scriptures are read in church. He is present, finally, when the Church prays and sings.[18]

This broadening of emphasis has significant implications for the priest, who presides at the Eucharist. It lessens the exclusivity of focus on the ministry of the priest as a means through which Christ can be present in the liturgy, as it implies that his presence can come about through the ministry of other members of the Church as well. However, this is not an impoverishment of priesthood. It is, rather, an enrichment and affirmation of the *mystery* of ordination itself, which no longer needs to be seen in terms of 'power' to dispense other sacraments. Along with them, and along with other ministries, it is in itself a distinct making-present of the mystery, rooted in the incarnation of the Word. Like all engagement with God in the sacraments, it has about it elements of the unseen which are perceived other than by the physical senses. St Ambrose speaks of this when he says:

> Do not believe your natural sight only. What is not seen is more truly seen, for this is eternal, while the other is temporal. We see more truly what is not perceptible to the eyes but is discerned by the mind and the soul.[19]

In its conferring and its exercise, the ordained priesthood is a sign of hidden reality as well as a visible functional office. It is a *participation* in and not a complete or exclusive *identification* with the priesthood of Christ, the fullness of which is not within our grasp. Priests are not Christ himself (and neither is anyone else). Our *sacramental* relationship with God can only ever be provisional. In the world to come sacraments will cease, but in this world they are nevertheless a real, life-giving means of experiencing the love and mercy of God in a way that is ultimately beyond the capacity of the finest intellect and the deepest spirituality. They enable us to reach out of what we can see, feel, smell and hear, and heaven to reach in. We experience now but a foretaste of the full life of heaven as a reality of the Christian life. The priesthood does not define but is a part of this experience. It is not the summit of Christian perfection, but is woven into the rich tapestry of God's self-giving love.

Odo Casel wrote that baptism, confirmation and the Eucharist are

> the stages of complete engrafting into the body of Christ ... These three mysteries are therefore the most important and most necessary for the life of the church and each Christian.[20]

It is in the sacraments of initiation and the Eucharist that *all* are called and enabled to participate in the priesthood of Christ. Ordination is only properly understood in this context, in terms not of superiority or exclusivity, but of vibrant, complementary difference:

> The body of Christ is a living organism, not a dead heap of similar atoms: it has a variety of members with different functions, both in its final form and ... in the accomplishing of those of its tasks on earth which will come to an end with this world's time.[21]

The priest is given a share in particular gifts, and the place of the ordained priest in the mystery of the Church is defined by the fact of their *combination* and *focus* for a particular ministry of service.[22] Through that ministry, the excellence and richness of the gifts of the whole people of God may also be combined and focused for worship, for the building up of the body of Christ, and for the preaching, teaching and living of the gospel. Ordination places the ordained person in a sacramental and ministerial relationship with the whole people of God, and it is in the animation of this relationship that the mystery of God is disclosed and explored. In a similar way, baptism brings a new relationship with the whole Church in which the mystery of God is celebrated. The ordained person has already experienced this gift: ordination, a gift of service, builds on its foundations.

Priesthood and mystery in liturgy and life

Priesthood is rooted in the mysterious and life-giving power of the Holy Spirit. The Anglican ordinals show the Spirit to be at the heart of our understanding of ordination: 'Receive the Holy Ghost ... Send down the Holy Spirit.' Especially if we are involved in exercising some form of ministry, we can forget to acknowledge the Spirit's hidden work in ourselves, as well as in others. Those ordained to a ministry of the Spirit must therefore like every Christian trust also in the *hidden* purposes of

God, and believe equally in what is seen more properly with the soul than with the eyes.

It was such conviction that led Edward King, the saintly Bishop of Lincoln, when a professor of pastoral theology to write of 'the great mystery of the priesthood, and the greatness of the work it involves'.[23] King saw more deeply than many of his time that like the other sacraments, including baptism, ordination signifies something far more than the merely visible, functional or even symbolic. What is entrusted to the priest at ordination indeed has visible attributes in terms of function, but is ultimately wrapped up in and serves to disclose in a limited but gifted way the mystery of God. King attempted to convey something of this when he wrote to one about to be ordained priest:

> Just simply give yourself to God, never mind what you *feel*, your being weary or excited, or put out ... that will pass, and the great supernatural *fact* will remain. God bless you, and make you a priest according to His own will.[24]

For King, priesthood was before all else a gift of God, a work of the Spirit, and as such it cannot wholly be explained or categorized. Richard Meux Benson, the founder of the Society of St John the Evangelist, wrote to a newly ordained mission priest encouraging him to

> recognize the presence of the Holy Ghost, Whom we receive, as accomplishing in us the work of the priesthood, so entirely beyond all human power – at once miraculous in its extent, and mysterious in its character.[25]

Such language of mystery – even from King and Benson, two of the most impressive but very different Anglican priests of the nineteenth century – may seem to be unfashionable and unhelpful today when the Church is much concerned, and rightly, with the numbers, deployment and function of priests in a rapidly changing cultural and social setting. Robin Greenwood has contributed to this debate in his influential book *Transforming Priesthood*,[26] much as the contributors to *Europe without Priests?* have in the Roman Catholic context. To talk of ordained priesthood as something 'supernatural' and 'mysterious', however theologically justified and spiritually attractive, may seem in practice to be out of step with the realities and demands of the contemporary Church. This is in fact precisely the point, for the sacramental, mysterious, Spirit-filled, hidden-and-disclosed nature of priesthood must be taken ever more seriously if this ministry is to be seen as anything other than a function of committee-bound, money-driven church structures, enslaved by society instead of close to the stirrings of its heart in the prophetic freedom of God's service.

Priests feel and know themselves to be far more than mere institutional functionaries because their lives are rooted in the daily dying and rising with Christ that is at the heart of the life of the parish or other community in which the priest serves. This is typified in the liturgy. Priests do not preside at the Eucharist *only* because somebody has to, but because ordination in the Spirit has placed them in a particular relationship with the unending hymn of praise which is the worship of heaven. 'Therefore with angels and archangels, and with the whole company of heaven' is not a theological fantasy, but a description of what is actually happening in the liturgy. God calls and enables the priest to preside over the interface between that eternal worship and its earthly foretaste, in the re-presentation of the paschal mystery of Christ's self-offering, death and resurrection. The paschal mystery is disclosed in the lives of the whole people of God, but it is through the complementary ministry of priest and people that it is made present in the assembly of the faithful, and that the divine gift of *koinonia* is both given and most truly expressed. This central, most distinctive role of the priest is carried into everyday life, where the ordained servants of the people of God, as pastoral leaders of the community, so often find themselves in situations crying out for the reconciliation and healing that they proclaim in the word and that are made present in the liturgy over which they preside. The vestments are left in the church, but the sacramental sign of the priest in the liturgy is carried into the streets of the parish and makes itself known with unremitting power and vitality, as the people of God, including the priest, together celebrate what for Karl Rahner is 'the liturgy of the world'.[27]

Clothed from within

Once a priest has been placed in this sacramental, mysterious relationship with God's people, no amount of casual clothing or risqué language can wholly hide it. Even the most 'unreligious' people, even those most indifferent or hostile to anything remotely to do with the Church can often seem to see through the priest's essential humanity to the God who has given the gift of priesthood, even if their recognition is in the form of abuse. Indeed, something of the mystery of ordination might even be discerned in those who are no longer in active ministry. In Graham Greene's novel *The Honorary Consul*, Charley Fortnum recognizes in Rivas not only the revolutionary he has become but the active priest he once was:

> The man broke two eggs one after the other on the edge of the
> pan. As he held two half shells over the pan there was some
> thing in the position of the fingers which reminded Fortnum

of that moment at the altar when a priest breaks the Host over the chalice.[28]

Rivas has attempted to shed his identity as a priest by becoming a revolutionary and ceasing to have an active ministry, and yet to Fortnum his actions still reveal him to be one. The mystery of ordination still seems to mark him, even though he has exchanged the confessional for the rebel's hide-out. He serves as an example of priestly identity not needing to depend on external appearance or even on aspects of lifestyle, but rather on what is said and done in the sacramental relationship between priest and people in life and liturgy that is a participation in the mystery.

Outward appearance can only ever be at the service of this mystery: it can never give the priest identity in this sense, but the differing levels on which it operates are useful as a focus for a discussion of that identity. The relatively modern custom of wearing clerical collars, already fast disappearing in many European countries, is in many ways of relatively little importance beyond the level of superficial identification as some kind of ecclesiastical office-holder. There is no doubt that it can serve to reinforce a sense of priestly 'separateness', but there are of course many circumstances in which such overt, universally recognized identification is appropriate. Nevertheless, as every priest knows, it can serve both to facilitate and frustrate practical ministry. Almost all priests will have felt at some stage in their ministry that it might have been better to wear casual clothes on certain occasions, if only to get people to be themselves. It is important to admit that priests can neither dismiss the limited usefulness of distinctive clerical garb as an unspoken statement of their identity nor wholly rely on it as such. Wearing a linen collar and silk stock does not define the priest. In Anglican circles the type of collar and colour of shirt has unfortunately become for some a badge of churchmanship rather than a sign of a common understanding of priesthood shared by the whole Church and recognized in varying degrees by those on its fringes. Much more helpful is to realize that in some circumstances the very absence of such superficial signs has been the key to fruitful, self-sacrificing priestly ministry.

In his pair of books about Mexico during the suppression of religious practice in the 1920s and 1930s, *The Lawless Roads* and *The Power and the Glory*,[29] Graham Greene focuses on the persecution of the Catholic Church. Priests were primary targets in this persecution because the survival of the Church depended on their ministry. To avoid capture, they went to unprecedented lengths to conceal the fact that they were priests. Some married, and none dared wear distinctive clerical clothes, except for the mass vestments in secret. The most famous of these priests in real life was Father Miguel Pro, who is shown in a photograph of his execution wearing a suit and tie, his arms outstretched in the form of a cross as the trigger is pulled.[30] Greene's fictional version is the 'whisky priest' in *The Power and the Glory*, who takes refuge in alcohol, but whose attempts to disguise his priesthood nevertheless lead him inexorably to his own death. It is interesting to compare Keillor's Father Frank with these Mexican priests, for whom dress and lifestyle became the very means by which their identity could be concealed from their persecutors but continue to be revealed in their clandestine sacramental and pastoral ministry. The need to conceal themselves paradoxically stripped away the same misleading perception of priestly identity as something to do with appearance, which erects an unnecessary barrier between Father Frank and his temporary flock. The Mexican priests were able to carry on their ministry by making themselves look like lay people, but if they had *been* lay people, they would not have had that ministry, nor would they have been persecuted.[31]

It is tempting to latch onto such powerful imagery surrounding appearance and see in it the root of priestly identity, but in the end it is only imagery. The theological identity of these priests lies ultimately in the fact of their ordination in the Spirit. Although changing their appearance is practically useful and life-extending, it is not in itself the key to their identity as priests, because it is dependent on the demands of a particular setting in space and time. Whatever they *look like*, what they are *doing* as priests in relation to their people is no different from other priests anywhere in the world at any time and in any political and social circumstances. The drama of their particular situation does not increase or lessen the degree of self-offering and service, even though some became martyrs because of it. They did not have a special ordination for priests about to be persecuted, but were ordained in the same way as others before and after them, and filled with the same gift of the Holy Spirit. The Eucharist they celebrate with their people is the same Eucharist that is celebrated in a village church in Cornwall. The unconditional offering of themselves in the service of their people is of equal dignity to that of any other priest anywhere, whether or not it leads to death.

This universality is at the heart of the mystery of the priesthood, because it identifies with the one sacrifice of Christ, with the one mystery of his love veiled from our sight and yet made present reality at all times and in all places through the sacramental action of the Church and in our daily experience of dying and rising with him. His self-offering and death occurred in a particular place and at a particular time, and yet they are not tied to that place and time. In the particular life of grace to which they are called, priests make present that self-offering and death, and point to it in all who by baptism share in the priesthood of Christ. This is a role not of status, but of service, because it makes present something offered and given, not demanded and taken. It is a role determined not by being clothed from without by social convention or historical circumstance, but by being filled from within by the unchanging, unseen, mysterious power of God. St Ambrose was trying to convey this when he wrote in his treatise *On the Mysteries* to those who had been baptized:

> You saw there the deacon, you saw the priest, you saw the chief priest. Consider not the bodily forms, but the grace of the Mysteries ... [the priest] is an angel ... to be esteemed by you not according to his appearance, but according to his office.[32]

'Who do you say I am?'

There is a danger in emphasizing the spiritual, sacramental dimension of priesthood, rooted in the mystery of God as revealed in Christ, not only in that the primacy of baptism may be obscured, but that ironically we may not pay enough attention to the fullness of its Christological aspect. Indeed, the latter can help to avoid the former pitfall. Priesthood must be understood in relation to Christ's humanity as well as to his divinity, both of which are at the heart of the paschal mystery celebrated by the whole Church. As the quotation from St Matthew's Gospel at the beginning of this chapter implies, a central theme of the Gospels is the identity of Jesus Christ – perhaps it is *the* central theme. Like John the Baptist before him, he is questioned about it. Sometimes he wants to know who people think he is, and sometimes he wants to conceal his identity. Similarly, priests are often asked who they are and what they think they are doing; priests are concerned about how they are regarded in their parishes; priests sometimes want to conceal the fact that they are priests, perhaps even from themselves. Whatever the temporal and practical circumstances, there is an essential and indispensable theological link between their identity and the identity of Jesus Christ. His own role is only gradually and unevenly revealed to those around him, in his words and in his actions, and in moments of enhanced perception granted to certain of his followers, as at his transfiguration. The disclosure of his identity is carried out wholly in the context of service. It is for others that he has come into the world, and it is for others that he will allow his life to be taken. There is nothing about his outward appearance that particularly distinguishes him from any other Jewish man of the time. That is the point. His life can be taken because he is fully and unambiguously human, and yet it is the fullness of both humanity and divinity in him that identify him as the Christ. He empties himself of divine power while remaining the incarnate Word, and he takes on himself the identity of a human being, with all the risk of exposure to pain, fear and temptation.

It is the combination and focus of divinity and humanity that identify Jesus Christ as our Lord and Saviour, and it is an identity that cannot be separated from the mystery of God from which it flows and of which it is an aspect. By becoming human, Christ transformed humanity, and so we humans cannot identify ourselves without identifying him who has transformed the very basis of our being. If Christ has not transformed our humanity by taking it on himself, by surrendering his life, and by rising again, then to talk of his presence with us now is delusion. If Christ is not fully God and fully human, alive now in his Church, baptism is empty and meaning-less, because we believe that by it we share in his death and resurrection and that it is itself a sharing in his divinity and his humanity. By the same token, ordination cannot have meaning unless we can embrace and hold fast to the identity of Christ in whose name it is given and lived. We cannot say who the priest is unless we can say who Christ is. Christ's humanity is crucial to his identity, and this means that the priest's humanity cannot be set to one side, but must be seen as at the heart of what it means to be a priest.

Priesthood, humanity and mystery

The priest is a disclosure of the paschal mystery of Christ, rooted in his divinity, and yet at the same time is a priest because of humanity, not in spite of it, and must not cultivate a distorted aloofness from the everyday lives of those for whom the ordained ministry exists.[33] To do so would be to deny the humanity of Christ. The priest, however, unlike Jesus, is exposed not only to temptation, but also to the real possibility of giving in to it. The person St Ambrose esteems as an angel can very easily fall but, as the eighteenth-century Anglican bishop Thomas Brett wrote, this capacity is part of what priesthood means:

> Those therefore who would have priests to be angels, or to discover no infirmities which are common to all mankind, do not rightly consider what is best for themselves; for if priests were exalted above human nature, they could never be so sensibly touched with the infirmities of others. If they were angels, they would not know how to make allowances for the weakness of the flesh and blood, and would be ready to expect that the people should be angels as well as themselves. Neither could they, with that earnestness and fervour, offer up their prayers and intercessions for the sins of others, when they had none of their own to beg pardon for.[34]

The persecuted Mexican priests were ultimately identified by their sacramental actions and pastoral care, not by their appearance. The identity of the priest is therefore primarily to do with what is done, not what is seen, for appearances can be deceptive, and were deliberately so in 1920s Mexico. But there is nevertheless a link between the priest's actions, appearance and the need to remain fully human, a vulnerable child of God born of water and the Spirit. Garrison Keillor's Father Frank wears yellow shorts and drinks a spirit of a very worldly kind, but he also wears vestments and presides at the Eucharist. A priest known to the writer never wears clerical dress because he believes that if a priest has a distinctive appearance, it is only when he presides at the Eucharist that it has any relevance at all. His role there is enough to sustain his priestly identity when away from the altar, although not of course away from the context of the Eucharist, which is to do with our everyday lives as well as with what we do in church on a Sunday. Walking along the High Street in jeans and a casual shirt, he is still the priest and known to be so, because of the role he exercises in the liturgy and in pastoral care, but he is also a human being.

Often, as with Greene's Father Rivas, it is other people who wish to deprive priests of their humanity, not priests themselves, because of the culture that has been acquired from the once-official theological emphasis on the priest's separateness and spiritual superiority, and which for the people of Lake Wobegon makes Father Frank so hard to accept. The legacy of this is the fact that many people *expect* the priest automatically to be their spiritual and behavioural superior, and often *believe* it always to be the case: the priest carries the burden of 'an official saint, and an actual sinner', as Austin Farrer brilliantly remarked.[35] The reality may therefore be the exact opposite, and some priests may more truthfully be, in the acerbic phrase of Martin Thornton, 'Graceless, spiritless, non-praying worldlings'.[36] And of course, tragically, they may seriously abuse not only the gift given them by God, but also the trust placed in them by the Church and by their people. Nevertheless, when the priest does something of a mild nature to confound the stereotype, the reaction can be one of genuine surprise or muffled hostility, as with Father Frank. On an ecumenical pilgrimage, a non-Anglican participant said that she was disappointed to have heard one of the Anglican priests swear. Right or wrong, this will immediately bring to the minds of many priests the overdone, embarrassed apologies of those who use an expletive in their presence, as if that particular section of vocabulary is totally outside the priest's experience, not to say usage! In a similarly trivial but equally revealing incident, two priests eating ice creams while wearing clerical attire provoked the comment, 'Oh, so you're human after all!' There is clearly a very delicate balance, and a constantly shifting set of images and perceptions.[37] The temptation is to go to either extreme of 'priestliness' or 'worldliness', or to see priesthood as something that can be discarded and taken up at will:

> There is a danger of the English priest discarding his status – or trying to – on holidays, days off, and recreation: a priest at the altar and a layman on the beach, a priest in the pulpit and a layman in the pub. The extreme sacerdotal schools avoid this error only by tending towards another; in spite of Christ the Carpenter and three-quarters of his saints, they look on menial work as unbefitting their state: the holy sacerdotal hands must not be defiled by a spade or a spanner – let alone a cricket bat. Meanwhile the English parson farms his glebe, cleans his car, and digs his garden, not because it is permissible but because it is part of his job, because he has to live in the closest sacramental relation with the world for which he pleads. Christ was High Priest only because he was God-Man.[38]

The language and certain points of ecclesiastical culture may be dated, and the perspective rather narrow, but Martin Thornton isolates precisely both a dilemma of priesthood and the reason why this dilemma must be embraced not as a problem or theological weakness of priesthood but as a fundamental aspect of the priestly life. This is not a new idea: George Herbert saw that the priest

> when a just occasion calleth him out of his Parish (which he diligently, and strictly weigheth, his Parish being all his joy, and thought) leaveth not his Ministry behind him; but is himself wherever he is.[39]

The tension priests experience within themselves and at the hands of others is itself a revelation of the tension in Jesus Christ's identity, between the fully divine being who was before the world was made, and the finite, tempted human being struggling to convey the message of ultimate truth. Jesus met with many different reactions to his presence, appearance and message, some nearer the mark than others. Even those who became his closest followers often failed to understand or misinterpreted his words and actions. Those who were most hostile to him, on the other hand, were very often the ones who came nearest to the truth, and wished to do away with him because of it. All of these reactions, whether justified or not in terms of factual accuracy, are relevant to the process of discerning his identity and are approaches to the mystery. The baptized Christian is, of course, faced with a range of perceptions in his or her life, like the priest. Both are who they are because of who Christ is.

Attempts by others to question the priest's role and identity should be seen in the context of the search for Christ in one another, just as pastors themselves look for Christ in those whom they serve. As Austin Farrer said in another sermon, priest and people must 'be Christ' to one another: 'We must be Christ to others, they can be Christ to us, we can never be Christ to ourselves', and priests must recognize 'the Christ in [others] who will draw to himself the Spirit he has placed in us, for the glory of God the Father'.[40] The priest, then, simply by being a priest, can be a focus of Christ's presence, and the agent of his search for us and ours for him.

This does not necessarily require immense spiritual proficiency, but a willingness to be used by God in his service, to be changed by the mystery and to be 'crushed by the Glory' if need be. The priest does not need to take refuge in the trappings of ecclesiastical culture nor even to be inordinately eccentric. The mystery of God is infinite, and yet conveys a simplicity which the centuries have tried to clothe in ill-fitting garments of social conformity and political expediency. Thomas Merton believed that he was one of the most unlikely people to have become a priest, and set great store by the sheer ordinariness through which the mystery of God is made present in the priest and in the world, and with which the priest is identified with Christ for the task of recalling others to the same source of their identity:

> The greatest thing that happens in priestly ordination is the most ordinary. That is why Holy Orders is, in its conferring, the simplest of the Sacraments. The Bishop, saying nothing, lays his hands upon the head of the ordinand. Then he pronounces the words of a prayer and the new priest receives the grace and indelible character of the priesthood. He is identified with the One High Priest, the Incarnate Word, Jesus Christ.[41]

The priesthood, for all its multilayered imagery and rich potential for disclosing and doing God's will, is in essence a particular living out of the fundamental simplicity of the gospel within the baptismal framework of the Church. It is rooted in the mystery of the God who transcends space and time, and yet has no meaning apart from the manifestation of that mystery in space and time in the confinement of a young girl's womb and nailed high on a cross. Its special task and immeasurable privilege is to be, sometimes unwittingly, a focus of others' search for this mystery, and to serve them in the liturgical re-presentation of it, day by day, week by week, year by year. The priest is ultimately called to be transparent, but usefully so, like a pair of glasses. Sometimes we need glasses in order to see more clearly: when using them, it is not the glass of the lens we see but that at which we are looking and with which we are engaging. Priests are called to be a particular kind of lens (and there are other kinds) through which our Lord may be seen all the more clearly by those to whom he beckons. The glass may sometimes be cracked, the magnification may not be as much as we would like, but the view is unmistakable, and heralds perfect vision in the kingdom.

The special calling to priesthood, understood as a mystery, depends on something in apparent contradiction to it: all the baptized are a royal priesthood. Christ liked to hold contrasting truths in tension. Seen in that light, the big question becomes not, 'What is a priest?', but 'What is the link?' Our search begins in an unlikely place …

2
Screen Idol

JOHN GRIBBEN CR

For all of us our jobs may seem pretty dull when we are doing them, and may well sound interesting and exciting to somebody else. We are all inclined to daydream about the different kind of life that we might have had, of the things that we would have done 'if only' ... When I was registrar at the College of the Resurrection, Mirfield, I can remember processing an application form and seeing the details of the applicant's occupation – a submariner! It sounded so wonderfully adventurous and romantic, especially to someone like me who, at that time, spent the greater part of the day behind a desk doing administrative jobs and marking essays. It evoked memories of all those films about submarines, the terror of depth charges, the fear of being trapped at the bottom of the sea.

This is an age when daydreams are made for us. Cinema and television dramas bring us into worlds where anything is possible. We can sit on the edge of our seats while Indiana Jones eludes certain death from crocodiles, snakes and sinister Nazis, or James Bond, fresh from the wreckage of a blazing ship, settles down in the life raft to be friendly with some beautiful girl. It is from such daydreams that the cult of the screen idol was born. Rudolph Valentino, back in the days of the silent film, was probably the first such idol. His star role in *The Sheikh* even today is an icon of the love-maker and for several generations a woman in love would refer to the man of her dreams as 'my sheikh'.

A screen idol drew the crowds because he or she had something which could touch the heart, produce the tingle factor, make us laugh, make us cry, make us gasp, make us squeamish. The heart-throb, the pathetic clown, the swashbuckling hero, the *femme fatale* – each had their special appeal. Sometimes this was the talent for which the film was just a backdrop – such were the great singer, the marvellous dancer, the Fred Astaire, the Betty Hutton. With others again it was undiluted sex appeal: Marilyn Monroe, Sabrina, James Dean. In the pre-television age we were prepared to queue in the cold and rain out of devotion to a particular hero or screen goddess – theirs were the shrines that we visited, and theirs the favours we sought as we left behind a world bereft of imagination, excitement or beauty.

What is the explanation for this devotion – to a Valentino whose death and funeral caused mass hysteria; a Doris Day whose fresh sweet face and golden bobbing hair could leave you light-hearted and with a sense of well-being; Harpo Marx who could wring laughter and tears from the most heartless of audiences; Bela Lugosi whose gentlemanly Dracula sent shivers down the spine? I know that I show the signs of age by the examples that I use (and even *I* don't remember Valentino!) and that a younger devotee would be enamoured of Demi Moore or Whitney Houston and that there are magnificent actors from the 1980s and 1990s who could illustrate my point just as clearly, but I speak from my own age of dreams.

They were good actors and were loved for their entertainment value, but it wasn't as the flesh and blood human beings that they were popular or loveable. Doris Day, who is the perfect image of domestic stability and married bliss, has had more than her fair share of pain and disaster in her home life. Chaplin, the little man who is always put upon, was in fact a very hardheaded businessman, and in real life there was nothing romantic about Valentino.

What makes a good screen idol is not just their ability to act but their ability to act *for me*. It is not so much that I admire Indiana Jones as a great adventurer. Rather is it that Harrison Ford can make me feel that it's me out there experiencing the tension, the fear, the relief. When the violins reach their crescendo and in close-up the heads move together for the kiss of the evening, it's not Clark Gable or Kevin Costner but me who is the great lover about to live happily ever after. The screen idol vicariously lives the romance, the excitement, the nobility, the dignity and sometimes even the anarchy that is in my heart but beyond my powers of expression.

This is not just a good trip into virtual reality. However unlikely the plot, however thin the story, this identification with the actress or actor is really an activity of the soul because it is the things that they represent that I identify with – opening me up to the possibility of being noble, courageous, free. On the screen the star is able to represent truth, beauty, goodness, and to draw us into those virtues for ourselves.

When Olivier makes the St Crispin's Day speech, I want to be English, to save my country. When Buster Crabbe faces the Emperor Ming, I want to be on the side of right, I want to oppose evil. When I weep at *Mrs Miniver* or *The Hasty Heart*, it is because Greer Garson or Richard Todd have taken me into the regions of the soul where matters of life and death stand before me, and I reflect on them in a way that Descartes or Socrates could never have moved me to. Even the villains and the baddies present me with the dilemmas of life, with the choices between good and evil, with the certainties of judgement, with issues of integrity.

In a way, that is what the Christian priest is called on to do for the people of God in the parish. This priestly ministry involves the priest in being a representative, an icon, a curtain-raiser: representing the truth of Christ to us, introducing us to the things of salvation. Just as James Stewart could stand in the courtroom in *Mr Smith Goes to Washington* and make us feel revulsion against graft and corruption, so by portraying the gospel the priest can lead us to a vision of the 'kingdom of heaven and his justice'. The priest can lead us into anger against injustice, into pity, compassion and mercy, and can show us that the kingdom of heaven is like ...

The function of a priest of the Church is to help the Christian congregation become more fully what it is already – a people who love and serve God. We might say that in this ministerial role the priest is the close-up that draws us into the action. By being our representative at the altar, the priest leads us into the one body of Christ that offers the sacrifice of praise and thanksgiving to the Father. It is this person who says the words, but our hearts and minds go with him.

Screen idols act out the drama for me through a mixture of hard work and talent, skill, good looks and charisma. They identify with the characters they are playing, and I in turn identify with them. Their ability to be a representative depends on how good this mixture is. In the religious drama of the liturgy the celebrant represents the mystery to me and makes me part of it, not because of any ability to act but because of the authority endowed upon that person by their calling, and recognized in them by the Christian congregation. This recognition is expressed in the ordination service where, by rite and ceremony, the ministerial calling is accepted by priest and people together. Among these rites and ceremonies one of the most potent symbols is the moment when the newly ordained person is vested. To invest someone is to put clothes upon them, but it carries with it the idea that they are being clothed with the office that they are to bear. 'Endue thy ministers with righteousness; and make thy chosen people joyful.' In the Old Testament the robing of the high priest indicated the representative nature of his priesthood:

> And you shall make a breastplate of judgment, in skilled work; like the work of the ephod you shall make it; of gold, blue and purple and scarlet stuff, and fine twined linen shall you make it. It shall be square and double, a span its length and a span its breadth. And you shall set in it four rows of stones. A row of sardius, topaz, and carbuncle shall be the first row; and the second row an emerald, a sapphire, and a diamond; and the third row a jacinth, an agate, and an amethyst; and the fourth row a beryl, an onyx, and a jasper ... So Aaron shall bear the names of the sons of Israel in the breastplate of

judgment upon his heart, when he goes into the holy place to bring them to continual remembrance before the LORD. (Exod. 28.15–21, 29, RSV)

When the high priest went into the sanctuary he wore a breastpiece over his vestments. This breastpiece contained twelve precious stones on which were engraved the names of the twelve tribes of Israel. This was to symbolize that when he stood before God's altar he bore the people of God on his heart. He stood as their representative, he prayed in their name and he carried back to them God's word and God's will. The ordination hymn 'Pour out thy Spirit from on high' applies this theme to the Christian priesthood:

Wisdom and zeal and faith impart,
Firmness with meekness from above,
To bear thy people in their heart,
And love the souls which thou dost love.

At ordination the priest takes on responsibility for the people of God, representing them at the altar, bearing them in his prayers. This means that, in a sense, there is a priestly spirituality. It is not that here there is a special Christian, much less a better one than anybody else. It is just that the priest's prayer life is conditioned by the responsibilities given.

But there is also another way in which the priest is a representative – in being sent to a particular place in order to represent Christ there. The priest, putting on the stole, should remember three things.

First, when the stole is worn across the neck it symbolizes a yoke or a halter. It is a reminder that the priest is to bear the burden of Christ – an easy yoke and a light burden, when borne in love. But it does mean that they are not their own person any more. It is no longer possible to say, 'I don't want to do that, the Church can't ask that of me, I want my freedoms, I want fulfilment, I've got my rights.' Before anyone sets out on the path towards ordination they should reflect that they might be asked to give up everything.

Second, the stole also symbolizes the towel with which Christ washed the disciples' feet. To be a priest is to be an outward sign of Christ the servant and that does mean being a servant both in the parish and to the world. It is an evangelical sign – it speaks of Good News – and it is an effective sign for, where it is performed, people will see the gospel in action. It is not that the priest is to be the only servant in the parish or a more enthusiastic servant than other Christians, but it is that this service should enable others, each in their own place, to represent Christ the servant to a world in need of a vision of love.

Third, the stole is the vestment of angels. In the Greek version of St Matthew's Gospel, the angel who announces the resurrection is described as wearing a white *stolas*. The gospel that we are called to preach is everlasting, it is heavenly and it is full of joy. We bring good tidings of great joy. The gospel, of which the priest is the official representative and which makes all the people of God priestly, is a gospel of healing and reconciliation, bringing heaven into a broken world where hell once reigned.

In the Christian Church there is only one priest in the full sense of the word. Only Christ can lift the veil of human limitation and death and take us into the presence of the Father. Christ is the only priest, Christ alone can be the sacrifice that makes our at-one-ment with the Father possible. What happens in ordination is that the Church gives to the priest the authority to represent Christ's priesthood sacramentally. As Christ is the sign and sacrament of the Father's love, so the Church is the sacrament of Christ's presence in time. What he did once for all in history the Church makes significantly available to me today, and the Christian ministry is the agent of that significance. The priest is a sign of the gospel. By preaching that gospel, by celebrating the Holy Communion, by telling us of Christ's forgiveness when we confess, by ministering to the sick and comforting the troubled, this priest will be raising the curtain so that we can see the love of God.

When Christian ministers lead us in the Eucharist, they are leading us into the mystery, they are involving us in the truth. They are lifting the curtain, they are leading us to Calvary, to resurrection, to the last day, when all our joys and sorrows will be received and blessed by our Father. This is *our* celebration as much as the minister's, and we give praise to God that by this means we can participate now in all the work that Jesus did for us when he communed with his disciples 2,000 years ago. As the Church of England's liturgy for Maundy Thursday puts it:

At the Eucharist we are with our crucified and risen Lord
We know that it was not only our ancestors,
But we who were redeemed
and brought forth from bondage to freedom,
from mourning to feasting.
We know that he was with them in the upper room
so our Lord is with us here now.[1]

The leader of the Eucharist has no supernatural powers by virtue of their calling, and they are not magically changed into someone in possession of heroic virtue or strength. They are still just Fred or John or Marlene – weak, sinful, loveable, foolish, just like the rest of us, because the God and

Father of our Lord Jesus Christ delights to come to us by the means of earthly things. He comes to us in the waters of baptism. He comes to us in bread and wine. He comes to us by means of anointing when we are sick, and through the words of absolution when we are burdened by guilt. He comes to us through the ministers, the frail human beings that he has ordained to preach the gospel and to serve the kingdom.

However, there is more to be said. Just as somehow the film star is able to raise us above ourselves and turn us into heroes or lovers or clowns, so too the ordained priest touches each of us and raises us to the priestly status. The priesthood of the minister enables the whole Church to be what it was called to be – a holy people, a nation of priests. And don't just take my word for it, listen to what Leo the Great says about it. Speaking of his ordination to the episcopate he says:

> But it is also a gracious and religious thing in you that on the day of my consecration you rejoice as for an honour that is your own. Thus the one sacrament which confers the high-priest-hood is celebrated in the whole body of the Church. When the oil of consecration is poured, the grace flows more abundantly over the higher orders indeed, but it flows unsparingly too over the lower.[2]

This is what Bishop Lindsay Urwin meant when at the Caister Conference 1997 he said that we are a 'mitred people'. We all share in the priesthood and in the apostolic ministry. We do so in the first place by virtue of our baptism, as Leo says in the same sermon:

> In baptism the sign of the cross makes kings of all who are reborn in Christ, and the anointing of the Holy Spirit conse-crates them priests. So, apart from the obligations of our ministry, any Christian who has the gifts of rational and spiritual understanding knows that s/he is a member of a king-ly race and shares in the priestly office.

We do so in the second place because those who have ordination conferred on them by the whole Church are called to help individual Christians and congregations to be what they are – the praising people of God. So when we gather round the altar of the Lord, we are drawn into a drama. Led by one priest we all concelebrate, we all plead the one true, pure, immortal sacrifice. There should be nobody 'just in the pews'. We are all in the cast. And in this drama we all become sacraments of the 'real presence', we become the means by which Christ's love shines out upon the world:

Christ shines through the sacraments, as through transparent bodies, without impediment. He is the Light and Life of the Church, acting through it, dispensing of His fulness, knitting and compacting together every part of it; and these its Mysteries are not mere outward signs, but (as it were) effluences of grace developing themselves in external forms.[3]

I write as an Anglican and a catholic and therefore with a particular interpretation of ministry and of who may minister. However, what I have said could be applied to any man or woman who has been authentically called and accredited to lead a Christian community. The expectations of some communities will be different from mine and therefore the form of the drama may well be different but still the curtain will be lifted on the mystery of salvation. We still share in the drama of which the saints sing:

You were slain and by your blood you ransomed for God
saints from every tribe and language and people and nation;
you have made them to be a kingdom and priests serving our God
and they will reign with you on earth.
(Rev. 5.9f., *Celebrating Common Prayer*)

A tongue-in-cheek example, introducing serious questions about holiness, identification, and reciprocity. If priesthood of people and of minister are held in a tension, we now meet another set of contrasts when Indiana Jones is removed from the screen, and priests themselves are put there instead ...

3

The Priest in the Media Age

CHARLES PICKSTONE

There is no culture without the shedding of blood.
(Nietzsche, *The Genealogy of Morals*)

Every year in our borough, we have a People's Day, when an estimated 20,000 people from all over the borough converge on a large park on the edge of my parish to browse through stalls, displays, marquees, tents, wigwams and caravans, and to view performances by local children. Last time I attended, these included rather beautiful Indo-Chinese dancing, English folk dance, (interminable) Irish line dancing, Spanish dancing, a 'Grupo Folklorico', more Irish dancing, 'Shantuna' dancing, Vietnamese traditional dances, Korean dancing, 'Recuerdos de España' and 'Dagarti Arts' – and this was at just one venue of three at Lewisham People's Day. It was apparent from the racial identity of the girls and boys who performed and from the care with which their parents had either made up or purchased their costumes that each set of performers represented a different cultural sub-section of this typical London borough.

Among the many stalls, there was even a Church of England stall, situated not among the wigwam, 'mystical' section of People's Day (alternative therapies, magical arts, crystals and yoga) but between the Humanists and the Tenth Lewisham Scout Group. The chief attraction there was a cassock-unbuttoning competition but, as it was only a 17-button cassock and anyway there was no one inside it, it was rather a dull affair by comparison with some of the other displays.

To the casual observer, two familiar notions are powerfully reinforced by Lewisham People's Day. First, that today the Church is almost literally just one market stall set out in a great bazaar of faiths, cultural activities, para-religions and spiritualities, and how important it is, in such a competitive, free-market environment, to look to our laurels and give the best account of ourselves to those who come to look.

Second, it is important to understand how regularly almost every child in the borough is involved in performing, whether watching or taking part, whether at school or in church or here at People's Day. Performance is one of the key aspects of our way of life, and not just for children. As adults we spend a good deal of our lives watching or listening to people perform, whether on television, radio, cinema or elsewhere, and occasionally most of us have the chance to do it ourselves in one medium or another, even if just in a home-made video, on a phone-in radio programme or by having our photo in the local paper.

As a result, people today are almost uniquely self-conscious; even when there are no cameras present (and, of course, Lewisham People's Day bristled with cameras at every show), we are trained to be aware from earliest childhood of the impact that we are making. Thus, some would argue, our consciousness of ourselves is perpetually *mediated* – you might say we live in a *media* society; that rather than, on occasion, doing a little acting for other people, all of life is a performance, and we are constantly aware of ourselves as performers, and of our personalities, of the *personae* (masks) we adopt as we play our particular roles.

For some people, strutting one's part on the world stage in such a highly self-conscious way is just a bit of fun; but for others this is a deeply worrying phenomenon. Is it good to see ourselves as perpetually in a frame – whether framed by the television screen or the photo album? 'Framing' distances us from reality; it keeps the world at arm's length. Immediate experience, some would say (even of weddings and baptisms) is of little value compared to the mediated experience of the same events 'framed' by our television screens later. Being framed inevitably and necessarily distorts our experiences, as the double meaning of the word implies.

Which brings us to the priest. How far is the priest simply another performer in the media society, a performer with rather a stereotyped set of roles but, even so, one more familiar than many, thanks to the regular appearance of clergy in soap operas, television series, radio comedies and films? Almost anyone can think of at least six current television or radio series that are either about priests or have had priests in prominent roles. (At time of writing: *Father Ted, Ballykissangel, The Vicar of Dibley, EastEnders, The Archers,* the repeat of *Brideshead Revisited* – not to mention, going back a few years, *The Paradise Club, The Thornbirds, The Cathedral, Emmerdale, Barchester Towers, Pride and Prejudice, Priest*; and not forgetting Roger Royle's sterling work in that hardy perennial, *Songs of Praise,* that made him so household a name that for a time he was certainly better known than the Archbishop of Canterbury.) In Germany a few years ago, there were so many clerical series on television that the phenomenon became known as *die schwarze Welle* – the black wave.

Given how few of us there are, as priests we do receive the most extraordinary amount of media coverage for our numbers. Is the media's fascination with the priest a perversion, a corrupting influence, simply reinforcing the stereotyped ideas that people already have of clergy? Or does it correspond to a much deeper need, even in our secular society, for a depth, for a resonance in life, that people sense they lack and to which, in a way, however much they may mock us, they sense that we might represent some sort of answer or at least guide? Is there a desire, just occasionally, for a bedrock experience, a non-mediated experience of something genuinely outside or beyond ourselves?

The media

There is a great deal of glum talk about the media. Many theoretical works appear convinced that the media are propagating a sort of conspiracy: that television exists mainly to deliver a large enough number of people to the advertisers, or to ladle out a daily diet of soporific pap to the masses to keep them disempowered; and that we are all victims of our own media illiteracy and therefore unable fully to comprehend the techniques that programme makers use to keep us glued (against our better judgement) to the box.[1] However, it seems to me that these conclusions are superficial. Most people, in my experience, are highly 'media aware', and generally entirely conscious of the rather superficial manipulation of which television is capable. Many times these conspiracy theories seem little better than whinging.

Similarly with the priest: it is automatically assumed that if clergy appear in films or on television, this must be bad news for the Church because the media are corrupt. And yet what is the role of the priest in the media age? Are we merely useful figures to have around to marry and bury, or to be the fervent idealists who can bring a useful touch of intransigence or sexual conflict to spice up a soap opera? Is our media image simply that of sex-starved Catholic celibate or married Anglican buffoon? Or is there something more going on in the media's fascination with the priest?

This is something that should be of interest not only to clergy. Priests are priests within the context of the entire Church of the people. And so the treatment of the priest by the media is something that is important to lay people as much as to clergy. An unfair portrayal of the priest is demoralizing for the whole Church since, naturally, lay people will feel it to be an attack upon themselves also.

In this brief essay, I shall argue two points: that the media age is not nearly as bad for religion as it is cracked up to be (provided that we learn the rules); and that although the use of priests by the media is often stereotyped, it does betray a deeper sense of the genuine desire for God's presence, and that therefore the Church has a duty to get involved with the media – to risk supping with the devil, perhaps – for the sake of the gospel.

Two portrayals of priesthood

A good place to begin is with the portrayal of the priest on television, where, as we have seen, the clergy (and religion in general) make surprisingly frequent appearances. A recent study, 'Popular Religion on TV', viewed a random sample of half a dozen soaps, and found an 'explicit religious reference' every three and a half minutes; of these, only one in four was use of a religious term as a slang or swear word.[2]

The parish priest

'What's your dog called?' asked the Vicar of Dibley of a shorthaired young man bringing his vicious-looking dog to her new animal blessing service. A good deal was riding on the success of the day; she knew that her churchwarden was in collusion with the bishop to have her sacked if this innovation were a disaster.

'Satan,' replied the young man.

'Ah', says Geraldine, noticeably taken aback. 'Well, I hope he enjoys the sermon. Come to think of it, it's very brave of him to come at all.'

The Vicar of Dibley has had several successful series. Many would say that it is improving with time, featuring in one episode a wedding sequence which managed to put even *Four Weddings and a Funeral* to shame. The character played by Dawn French is, according to some, the best PR the Anglican clergy have had since before Derek Nimmo; she is the only television vicar who, by virtue of her status as a senior comedienne, is not made a fool of. All around her may be fools, including her rather slow friend Alice, who nicely sets her off (much like Julia Sawalha's Saffron in *Absolutely Fabulous*). She may have pictures of 'my boys' like icons on her wall (Jesus Christ and Cliff Richard). But she is remarkably human, and we laugh with her, not at her. The night before the animal service is particularly stressful: 'I do hope I don't do what I did last time,' she confesses to the camera – namely, binge on Crunchies and treacle. We observe her waking up the following morning, surrounded by Crunchie wrappers and an empty tin of syrup. It is a funny and yet also serious acknowledgement of the stress of priesthood. The series can hardly be seen as harmful, and underlying it is a positive image of pastoral priesthood lived out in not implausible situations of conflict by a fallible yet sympathetic human being.

There are few references in *The Vicar of Dibley* to the supernatural or to the miraculous. The picture is that of a flawed, deeply caring human being in conflict with other flawed characters in various pastoral situations. There is little suggestion of another world except for conventional ones: token shots of the Vicar 'at prayer'. This is probably the standard 'Anglican' model (and the Roman Catholic one in Ireland –

Father Ted – operates on much the same level, although *Father Ted* has a bleaker, more cynical twist).

The priest as outsider

There is a second common model of the priest on television – the priest as outsider. From the theological point of view, this model has more potential. The cosy world of comedies such as *All Gas and Gaiters* or *The Vicar of Dibley* does not leave much scope for the transcendent. Neither, in the more serious world of soaps, does the priest in *EastEnders*; Alex is big on social concern (if not on family values) – but we never see him at prayer and rarely in church. He seems motivated by entirely humane impulses.

On the whole, and with some notable exceptions, most of the more interesting priests on television, theologically, seem to be Roman Catholic. For much of the unchurched population of the UK, 'Catholics' are still seen as outsiders, their loyalty made doubtful by 400 years of negative propaganda and anti-Irish racism. They, therefore, are in a good position to represent another world which humdrum Anglicans cannot – we are altogether too familiar. In addition, given that British television is particularly good at portraying working-class culture and prizes down-to-earth robustness, the working-class origin of many Roman clergy is probably important in enabling them to be portrayed as strong and sympathetic characters.

My particular favourite is Frank Kane, the priest played by Don Henderson in the series *The Paradise Club* from the early 1990s – a city priest who had spent his life in a tough, working-class parish in the north and now, on the death of their mother and seeking respite from the Church (some sort of betrayal is alleged), has come down to London to help his brother run a nightclub in a seedy part of South East London. The brother is a smooth and likeable villain (played by Leslie Grantham seeking to escape his role as Dirty Den in *EastEnders*). The priest is the epitome of a sort of street-cred holiness, an immensely attractive character, apparently gullible but actually canny as a serpent, who spends the series trying in vain to make his brother go straight. His holiness is never in doubt, even though we are led to believe that it is this down-to-earth holiness which has turned the Church against him.

Even with Roman Catholics, there is often tension between the down-to-earth parish priest and members of the hierarchy who seem to live a gilded existence, or who have sold their souls to middle-class sophistication. The most famous example must be the opening section of the film *Priest*, where an old priest rams a great crucifix through his bishop's sitting-room window from outside while the latter is taking a genteel afternoon tea – a gratifying moment for parish clergy of all denominations.

These 'rough' priests are rarely mocked on television except affectionately. Their persona works on two levels. On one level, they correspond to the need most ordinary people have for a priestly figure in their lives, whether as ideal father confessor or the voice of their conscience – someone who can believe the things they do not have courage for, and who keeps to the principles they can no longer afford. But at a deeper level, they are a symbol of people's needs for something 'other' – a representative of another world, a world that is not superficially immediate, or mediated by our expectations.

In my book *For Fear of the Angels* I analysed this need for the figure of the priest principally in terms of his sexuality, especially as portrayed by the mass media. With the 'sexual celibate' priest, those two great mysteries, sex and religion, come close together. The media – and, indeed, many of the great films, novels and plays of the later twentieth century, from perhaps Anthony Burgess' greatest novel, *Earthly Powers*, to David Hare's *Racing Demon* – play on the priest's sexuality, sometimes simply for its conflict value but sometimes, too, as a way of linking into the mysterious, transcendental side of sex which is one of the few routes into the genuinely holy that ordinary, secular people are open to.

But sexuality is only part of the equation. These priests are not the cosy purveyors of wholesome family fun days to their morally cautious faithful. This image of the priest is of someone who has encountered the demonic, shadow side of existence, who has wrestled with the void rather than piously staying at home sipping tea. A good example would be Carlo Campanati in Anthony Burgess' *Earthly Powers* (a thinly disguised portrait of Pope John XXIII), as at home exorcizing demons in remotest South East Asia[3] as hitting the bottle on the streets of Paris or gambling dangerously at Monte Carlo (and winning).

> The priest is someone who has looked on violence and come to terms with it, someone for whom the sugar coating of easy religious experience long ago yielded to an anguished and lonely exploration of the dark and dangerous territory where known ways fail. The mysteries of death, violence and suffering are his speciality, the desert (whether literally or the urban deserts of the back streets) his habitat. His celibacy is thus only a part of a life that has been disciplined, its energy channelled into an encounter with the unknown.[4]

Priesthood, like sexuality in Paul Ricoeur's memorable phrase, is the flotsam of a submerged Atlantis and is often so used by the media: a reminder of the great, inaccessible continents of ancient spirituality that are no longer available to our civilized, media age. Priests are one of the few classes of people in our present society who retain something of the symbolic value of this vanished world.

In an affluent society, relatively pain-free, these interior heights and depths are rarely scaled. For some reason never satisfactorily explained, they are more accessible to the outsider – in a society where the pain of being an outsider is generally too great to be bearable by anyone who has any option of belonging. The vocation to the outside is difficult to bear amid the blandishments and allurements of a society only too happy to clasp to its bosom with bonds of success, sales and money anyone who has even the likelihood of a vision of the holy to offer.

There is a sense in which the figure of the priest as outsider can be used by the media to represent this dim awareness of the power and presence of another world – the world of grace – and especially the priest on the fringes of society: the gay priest, the celibate priest, the priest who has looked on violence and come to terms with it, the priest who has made the deserts of the inner city their home.

Priesthood and sacred space

While the latter model may be the more attractive (at least, to those of a romantic disposition), for those of us who have to run parishes, pay our quotas and fill our pews it is encouraging to find a certain sympathy for our difficult task on television. But we turn now to a more general problem that affects the portrayal of priesthood in the media. Some would argue that precisely because we live in a world that is both affluent and dominated by the media, *any* treatment of priesthood by the media will inevitably be false. To understand this argument, we must first consider the notion of sacred space and its relationship to suffering.

Sacred space 1

The European visitor to the United States of America is always impressed by the great areas of land that have been saved from development and turned into large national or state parks. Flying over the Rockies, say from New York to San Francisco, is an unforgettable experience; in Europe, we are used to the sudden, sharp, rather trim Alpine peaks emerging snow-capped from pine forests that disappointingly quickly revert to fields and farms, but here there is mile upon mile, hour upon hour of messy and arid terrain.

These virgin areas are important to American national identity. Yosemite National Park, for example, dating from 1890, is a remote valley cut off by a range of hostile mountains which rise out of a lush carpet of trees. For a hundred years it has symbolized the great untamed forests and crags that moulded the American pioneer spirit; as Simon Schama points out in his book *Landscape and Memory*, these undeveloped areas are important both as reminding Americans of their frontier past and also as providing spiritual refreshment,[5] an image of quasi-religious power regularly used by the media, who emphasize the priest-like nature of explorers of the spiritual meaning of this virgin territory such as Thoreau. American sacred space is empty of humanity and of history.

For a European, by contrast – coming as we do from a continent where every square inch of territory has been fought over from time immemorial and thus fertilized by the blood of our ancestors – it is very strange to be confronted with these vast and relatively pristine wilderness areas. It makes the American landscape curiously amorphous. There is a sense of being in a place where nothing (from a human point of view) has ever happened: a sort of vacuum state that is extremely disturbing, for the cultural vacuum is also a spiritual one. It epitomizes a rejection – a rejection of old Europe, a rejection of religious dogmatism, a rejection, perhaps, of the hell that makes paradise envisageable.

Of course, as Simon Schama points out, the notion of Yosemite's being virgin territory is a myth: its distinctive quality of lush and ancient forest out of which soar the towering crags only exists because the Ahwahneechee Indians over countless generations regularly started forest fires to allow new growth to emerge. (He also points out that the name 'Yosemite' has nothing to do with grizzly bears, as the tourist guides suggest, but is a version of the Ahwahneechee Indian name for the white man: 'some among them are killers'.[6])

And yet, on a mythological level, the European reaction to Yosemite which Schama typifies does underline the importance of Nietzsche's dictum, quoted at the outset (itself remarkably similar – perhaps intentionally – to Heb. 9:22 RSV: 'and without the shedding of blood there is no forgiveness of sins'). Back in Europe, the quaint landmarks and two-star cultural sites that we photograph with our disposable flash cameras and Camcorders to make tapes we will never have time to watch, may now have become degenerate and mass-reproduced icons, but are rooted in meaning because they were bought with suffering. So many ghosts have imbued them with their blood.

One of the best examples of these cultural sites is what some would argue is the British equivalent of Yad Vashem (the Holocaust memorial in Jerusalem), namely the vast network of First World War burial grounds around the River Somme. Every mile along the front line where English, French and German troops confronted each other in 1916/17 (not to mention Canadians, Australians, South Africans and New Zealanders), from the Somme escarpment up to Belgium, there is another graveyard, large or small. A significant proportion of the British population have great-uncles or great-grandparents buried there, a whole generation of 17- and 18-year-olds. The arch at Thiepval is covered with the names of thousands whose bodies were never identified. It still attracts a steady crowd of visitors.

The sight of all these graves is appalling. It is also an encounter that leaves surprisingly many of those who visit with the indelible effect of having encountered the truly sacred. There are reports of whole coachloads of militantly adolescent boys awed into silence.

The effect of the war on those who participated was like nothing else. This can be seen particularly in the war's artistic legacy. Perhaps the greatest monument to the First World War is a little-known chapel at Burghclere, south of Oxford – the Sandham Memorial Chapel – which the great maverick English painter Stanley Spencer filled with frescoes that speak particularly powerfully for what they omit. The imagery speaks as movingly of the horrors of war as any Wilfred Owen poem.

No one but a lunatic could possibly wish again for those days – nor should nostalgic yearning for the days when life had 'meaning' lead us on to forget the appalling pain and suffering reported by war poets and painters. But it is interesting that a great wave of this sort of talk – a veritable obsession with death – had been fashionable in the late Victorian and Edwardian periods, and upon this the First World War undoubtedly fed. We recently came upon an exercise book of my great-grandmother's, in which she had beautifully copied out extracts from poems by Byron, Tennyson and others – all to do with death. (She herself died in childbirth in the 1890s.) Even the gentle German animal painter Franz Marc talked about the necessity of 'cleansing the Augean stables of old Europe' when the First World War broke out. (He died at Verdun in 1916.)

This pseudo-mysticism of death – perhaps itself a response to that proto-media age, the Victorian period – quickly evaporated under the heat of the entirely mundane pain of life in the trenches ('The old lie: *dulce et decorum est pro patria mori*'). Nonetheless, out of this *mêlée* came the sacred spaces of the First World War graveyards, and a great deal of poetry that has shaped our national consciousness, from Binyon ('They shall grow not old') to Owen; this was perhaps the last time that national suffering could trigger a sense of the collective sacred. The extraordinary communal response to Princess Diana's death was a pale echo of this once powerful phenomenon. By contrast, the bloodless mythology of the virgin space of US 'wilderness' areas becomes an affluent conceit.

Sacred space 2

Perhaps blood and priesthood are related more closely than it is fashionable to admit. Today, not only is our world more affluent, and collective suffering (as opposed to individual pain) relatively rare, but the world has been levelled by economics, which recognizes few boundaries, and by the media. In this flatter, media world, we have instant communication across the globe. Any significant emotional or cultural charge is instantly dissipated. The oxygen of publicity may be good for fanning local flames, but it more usually quenches all-devouring forces by putting them into perspective. Great historical movements become relativized and emasculated.

As a result, there can be no collective sacred space of which the priest is custodian, no charged arena of the collective psyche that the priest articulates and that gives the priest power. In today's world even the *Titanic* can be raised, the perfect image of how what had once been a mighty symbol for the entire Western world – a symbol that spoke of luxury, guilt, *hubris* ('the Pride of Life that planned her'), our ambivalent attitude to technology and sense of the uncontrollability of nature and of the judgement of God, the 'Spinner of the Years' – has been reduced to a rusting passenger ship, bits of which can be exchanged and traded.[7] If there is no sacred space, then both priest and Church lose their particular privileges. 'Issues of Life and Death, once the province of religion, are now apparently worked out in the public arena of Ramsay Street and Albert Square far more than behind the closed doors of any church, synagogue or mosque.'[8]

There are many who argue that searching for any sort of holiness or transcendence in our immensely 'flat', media-dominated world is doomed and that the whole priestly enterprise is finished. For example, S. A. Schleifer, writing from an Islamic perspective, argues that

> television is essentially anti-meditative and has extreme difficulty handling religious material … In dealing with people whose spirituality may be strikingly evident in a personal encounter, television is unable to picture what is there, 'no iconic sense of the inner essence is revealed'. We cannot 'see' the saint via video. Such media can only simulate the image without its invisible aura of spiritual grace.[9]

Jean Cover, in an essay in the same collection, is highly critical of the use of religious imagery in advertising. 'Sacred symbols have been removed from their religious contexts to give a spurious feeling of transcendence and sacredness to a "theology of consumerism".'[10] However, while it must be admitted that adverts may perhaps cheapen religious symbols, they are not necessarily bad for priests, who are often treated better by advertisers than by the writers of soaps who generally enjoy playing on the hypocritical piety of the clergy.[11] There is currently a rash of stylish priests in television advertisements, including a memorable young woman, smartly dressed, who does not want vaginal thrush to spoil her big day: officiating at a wedding service.

The argument seems to go as follows: one of the prime functions of the priest is to be at the centre of sacred space.[12] But in a world where, thanks to the media, sacred space is at a premium it is not surprising that things are too cramped to allow of a sense of true priesthood: there is not enough sacred space to go round.

Many poets, especially, have been sensitive to this issue. R. S. Thomas, for example, uses the splendid image of a caged white tiger in his poem of the same name, *'glacial /eyes that had looked on /violence and come to terms /with it'*, as it paces round and round its cage, and breathing *'as you can imagine that /God breathes within the confines /of our definition of him, agonising /over immensities that will not return'*.[13] Similarly, back in the nineteenth century, Baudelaire used the image of the albatross as a metaphor for the poet in the contemporary world: the great winged bird, when caught by sailors, is trapped by the size of its wings and can be mocked; in the same way (and no doubt Baudelaire has Christian and Old Testament imagery at the back of his mind too), the poet is like this *'prince of the clouds, who roams the storm and mocks the archer'*,[14] but who, when in exile on the earth, is prevented from walking by his giant wings.[15]

Just as the white tiger, cramped in its cage, ponders immensities that will not return; and as the prince of the clouds looks simply ridiculous out of his natural habitat, struggling round the deck, so in the media world everything is immanent, anything transcendent suspect; there is no arena that can sustain anything of any profundity. Anything remotely unusual (a Hindu cow that weeps milk, a crying Madonna) is on television news the same day with a bevy of scientists to explain it all away.

Our information age puts all information on the same level and immediately trivializes itself. The mighty architecture of suffering, sickness, uncertainty and pain – which empowered the great medieval sacred spaces, which threw up the cathedrals and led men and women to invest in an exalted and transcendental otherworld – no longer has the same purchase. The implicit structures of today's architecture – functional and economic, structural and efficient, with a few curlicues thrown in for decoration – cannot bespeak the same transcendence. Small wonder that the media see priests, too, as the grounded albatross or caged tiger – fit subject for mockery, deprived of the natural habitat, of the sacred space, that would permit them to fly.

Should the Church use the media?

Despite its attractiveness, this argument is clearly specious. Few would gladly return to an age of so much pain, to a pre-technological world where even aspirin was unknown. A great deal of this talk is a romantic and possibly pernicious nostalgia in which religious people are often the worst offenders. Who would really like to live in the Middle Ages, especially when one considers that, to take one tiny example, even as recently as 50 years ago, the life expectancy of the average marriage was 15 years – thanks not to divorce but to mortality?[16] Like it or not, we live in a media age, and we need to accommodate to it to survive. The Church has a media image whether it will or no, and this is something that must be taken seriously.

Tunes of glory: Hollywood versus the Church

In the early 1990s, the Labour Party changed its stance on nationalization. For most of its history, the one thing that everyone knew about Labour was that it supported the public ownership of industry. But by August 1991, when the Conservative government announced the sale of another tranche of British Telecom shares, Labour had quietly dropped its commitment to renationalize the company. Peter Kellner, writing in the *Independent*, proclaimed this as the moment when 'British state socialism died'. However, Neil Kinnock, who was then leader of the Labour Party, asserted in an article in the *Director* in September 1991 that the 'huge majority of the Labour Party' had never believed in wholesale nationalization at all, 'but they were the tunes of glory that were coming out. Well, we've stopped that nonsense.'[17]

The Church, no less than the (old) Labour Party, is still tempted to sing those old tunes of glory, looking nostalgically back to some great age of faith (the 1930s? the 1880s? 1662? 1533? the thirteenth century?). We live in today's world and if we wish to survive we too must 'stop that nonsense'. The fundamentalist pursuit of a vanished pre-media world is a luxury we can no longer afford.

If one were a member of a radically unjust society struggling, against all the odds, for a fairer distribution of wealth, say, or for democracy or justice or human rights, one would certainly need to become some sort of fundamentalist (whether biblical or ecclesiastical) in order to buttress one's resolution to face imprisonment or even death for the sake of one's beliefs. But the armchair fundamentalism of so many in the Church in this country and (especially) in the United States can be simply a disguise to cover up intellectual laziness, a consequence of fear of the openness to insecurity that comes from having to work things out for oneself. The New Testament gives little support to the view that the Church should be chaplain to the moral majority.

One particular symptom of this armchair fundamentalism is a lazy mistrust of the media world. There is a state of war across the Atlantic between on the one hand the world of Hollywood, which takes every opportunity to parody and expose hypocrisy within the religious establishment and to show up the flaws of public, Christian morality; and, on the other, the Christian right, which threatens to use its vast numbers to boycott films of which it disapproves and thus to bring down the movie industry. As Michael Morris, a Dominican priest at the Graduate Theological Union in Berkeley and author of several books on film and theology, has pointed out, it is a great waste of talent and energy that two groups of people whose aims and interests are so similar, and who might so naturally be allies, should be at loggerheads. Many films make excellent sermons (who has not preached on *ET, Babette's Feast, The Mission, Dead Poets' Society*? I have heard a mean sermon preached even on *Highlander*). If only the Church could learn to overcome its mistrust of the media, it could use the media to its own advantage.

A small but excellent example of the latter is Wendy Beckett, the Roman Catholic sister who spends most of her life as a hermit in a caravan in East Anglia but who came to fame in the early 1990s as a commentator on first contemporary and latterly classical art, and whose programmes on television attract huge audiences. It is a splendidly symbiotic relationship: the television companies are able to film an elderly nun with a strong personality in full fig expatiating with glowing eyes in front of, say, a full-blown Renaissance nude – something which makes for compelling viewing – while Sister Wendy achieves the rare feat of drawing an audience of several million secular people to listen devoutly to the words of a nun in full habit.

And it is just not true, as many would claim, that Hollywood cannot portray genuine religious experience without mockery. One of the best recent examples of this is the 1996 film of Arthur Miller's play, *The Crucible*, starring Daniel Day-Lewis as the hapless Proctor – a thoroughly agnostic farmer of deep integrity, who is implicated in the general witch-hunt that divides his small village in Massachusetts.

Some girls from the village have been caught larking around naked in the forest and, to escape the severest penalties, have admitted to witchcraft. In token of their repentance, they go on to implicate other members of the village, generally on vindictive grounds, settling old scores. Proctor is implicated by a girl with whom he once had a brief affair in a moment of weakness and now rejects. He nobly refuses to take the easy option and confess to being a witch in order to avoid execution – and certainly not if it necessitates naming others as accomplices. He is sent to the scaffold at the end of the film by the witchfinders with two others – one of these a Mistress Goody, a very devout and pious old woman who will have nothing to do with the hypocrisy that is going on around her.

As the nooses are placed around their necks, the old woman begins to recite the Lord's Prayer. Proctor joins in, at first in defiance, but then with conviction, overcome by the power of the words. It is an extraordinarily moving moment as we see this secular agnostic experiencing a genuine conversion to Christianity before our eyes at the end of a Hollywood film – a true religious moment – a moment of grace.[18]

Of course, the noose tightens just before the end of the prayer, and Proctor is hanged before he can get to the 'Amen', martyred by Christian bigots. A Christ-like figure (the film makes the point by having the other two victims hanged one on each side), he brings about, through his unjustified death, the end of witchcraft-hunting. And, in a way, salvation comes to a small community, as Miller's postlude (surprisingly, not used by the film) makes plain.[19] Proctor is an enlightenment, media-age martyr who comes to Christ on celluloid. Perhaps the Church might do well to make friends with the media after all.

Rhetoric

Another reason for the Church not to fear the media age is simply that we are past masters at using the media ourselves. Back in the days of the early Church, rhetoric – the art of persuasion through speech – was one of the key areas of study of the ancient world. As Mary Charles Murray recently pointed out in an article on preaching in the early Church, the tradition of rhetoric found one of its principal exponents in St Augustine, who was schooled in rhetorical techniques.[20] Rhetoric became the approved means for Christian preachers to communicate with their audiences, pagan or Christian. (It seems that the early Church was less fastidious about using pagan techniques.)

Today, the techniques of rhetoric (which would now be seen as a branch of media studies) have been greatly refined; the best examples are those of television advertisers, which, when analysed, can be seen to exemplify many of the techniques of classical books of rhetoric. But the Church has been slow to avail itself of these techniques beyond the pulpit. Partly this is because of the sheer expense of the technologies of broadcasting and film, and partly because traditional advertising has largely allowed itself to be restricted to the rather narrow categories of products and services – neither of which the Church supplies in a traditional sense. Originally, rhetoric was about changing lives, and it may well be that the media will eventually catch up, producing untold opportunities for the Church.

And in any case, not to use the media is as important a choice in a media-aware world as to use it. Not even a Peter Mandelson-style spin doctor may be able to save the Church of England, but to be ignorant of the basic language of rhetoric is to risk sending out confused or even downright misleading signals to the rest of the world. Archbishops who wear cardigans on television may not be communicating the message they suppose. Like it or not, the Church has a media image and those who appear publicly in the name of the Church must learn the rules of the game.

The priest as prophet

Finally, however, let us suppose that not everything in the media garden is rosy; that there is a sinister side to the media that parallels the sinister side of our affluent society. Despite the ruthlessness of many journalists in their search for the truth, myths abound in our media age, and it is likely that some of them are dangerous. The priest is in as good a position as anyone to deal with them.

Perhaps, as some would claim, television – or simply the soap opera – really *is* the unifying force in our society, much as religion was for the Middle Ages; perhaps television producers *are* simply concerned to deliver up audiences to their advertisers (their real products are not programmes but audiences) so that we are entering a shallow, homogenizing, comfortable media society with a few token shocks, a 'secular-trivial world'[21] offering 'little pellets of sweetness',[22] and encouraging a sort of 'hedonistic fascism'.[23] Perhaps Neil Postman's thesis in his influential book *Amusing Ourselves to Death* is correct, that 'Entertainment is the supra-ideology of all ... television. No matter what is depicted ... the overarching presumption is that it is there for our amusement and pleasure', and thus that even news programmes, with their 'daily fragments of tragedy and barbarism', are simply there for our entertainment.[24] Perhaps, too, the increasingly monopolistic control of the media by powerful interest groups is unhealthy and will lead to truth's being ignored. And if media-framing is so pervasive that even our tenderest, most intimate moments with each other – those times when we might hope to be at our most genuine – are actually played out against a semi-conscious soundtrack that comes straight from Hollywood, then what are we in ourselves?

If these possibilities are true, then there is a sense in which the traditional vocation to the priesthood is one of the best ways of opposing the media blitz. Priests, even parish priests, are inevitably to some extent outsiders to society. Priests have a vocation to a particular ecstasy, an *ecstasis*, a standing outside, which puts us in a good position both to challenge predominant forces, but also to be in solidarity with others as they are thrown out too. Even if communal suffering is uncommon in an affluent society, for many people life is not at all comfortable. Contrary to the advertisers' blandishments, tragedies take place daily; not just the dramatic ones of cancer or AIDS but unemployment, redundancy, mid-life crises (half the middle-aged male population appears currently to be on Prozac), family breakdown, bereavement, poverty, bad education or just a general sense of failing in one's duty to be fulfilled – the list goes on endlessly. All these conspire to push people out of the cosy, media-framed and understandable world.

The parish priest, however, is the outsider – imposed upon a community by will of the bishop, a person 'with no employer upon earth' in the words of a recent Appeal Court ruling[25] – who therefore does not fall into the usual contract culture, and who does not fear redundancy (but neither do they enjoy the usual recourse against an employer if things go wrong). Similarly, the enforced near poverty of a priest (especially if their partner is not in paid employment) results in their not being able to compete on the consumer scale with others. All this means that as an outsider, the priest must depend on grace to accept what Dorothee Sölle calls the *Unverfügbarkeit* – the non-negotiability – of life, that which cannot be manipulated by the media.[26]

The priest, therefore, is one of a small band who can act as rebel as in the conformist media world. Television may tend to domesticate life; the priest has access – often involuntarily – to the highly undomesticated great white peaks of solitary experience. Such a person may not (should not?) be media-friendly, but will be able to act as figurehead for those who live lives of quiet sacrifice, suffering and self-denial, those who through the reality of their lives puncture the anodyne clouds of narcotic pap served up by the media which, though in themselves harmless enough, can like any other narcotic prove dangerously addictive.

The priest must set up his stall alongside the spiritualists, crystal-sellers and faith-healers, alongside the ecowarriors, animal liberation and social action groups, making strategic alliances where possible, exposing spiritual bunkum where necessary, trusting that by the grace of God, his or her hold on reality is attractive enough to those who are searching to draw them in. The priest as prophet can exercise a check upon the potentially overweening power of the media, a check that will, of course, be ignored or ridiculed at the time. But then we are used to crucifixion.

If the media can be blisteringly honest, how often do the People of God themselves have the chance to be so? ...

4

A Word from One of the *Laos*

MARGARET SELBY

> Let him also weep, the priest of God, and he will see that the
> hearts of his listeners tremble in answer to him … Whoever
> has no faith in God will have no faith in God's people, either.
> But whoever acquires faith in God's people will also behold
> his holiness, even though previously he had no faith at all.
> Only the people and its coming spiritual strength will convert
> the atheists among us … [1]

One of the most moving experiences of theatre that I have ever had was
at the Crucible in Sheffield. It was a performance of one of Shakespeare's
great tragedies. For some reason which I do not remember, we sat in the
front row of the stalls, before the low apron stage. To be so close almost
guaranteed that we would feel part of the action. However, this was greatly
added to because the only backcloth was a wall made entirely of mirror.
This meant that we not only observed the tragedy as it was played out, but
actually observed ourselves as part of it, as we saw our own reflections in
the mirror behind the players.

For me this has become an icon of the Eucharist. The Eucharist, if it
is to spell out to the gathered Church its true nature, has to be not only
the action of the priest, with or without their coterie of servers, but also
it has to be the action of the whole people of God. What we celebrate is
not only the whole story of God's dealing with his universe, from its
creation to the final consummation of all things, but at each celebration
we celebrate our ingrafting into the story of salvation, our being made
new, our lives lived through God, and for him and for his world. As we
take part in the Eucharist, the priest must see their own reflection in the
laity and the laity must always see themselves reflected in the action of
the priest. There has to be a mutuality, an inter-dependence, a mirroring,
a reciprocity, if the underlying meaning of the twin vocations to the lay
and the ordained life is to be understood.

This demands a mutuality of respect, 'in honour preferring one another'
(Rom. 12.10, AV), a sense that the Spirit is equally present in all, even if
for different tasks and vocations. This carries with it the insight that, in

order to do this, we must not 'exaggerate' our 'real importance' (Rom. 12.3, *Jerusalem Bible*), or as Paul wrote to the Philippians:

> There must be no competition among you, no conceit; but everybody is to be self-effacing. Always consider the other person to be better than yourself, so that nobody thinks of his own interests first but everyone thinks of other people's interests instead. In your minds you must be the same as Christ Jesus. (Phil. 2.3–5, *Jerusalem Bible*)

This may seem too obvious to be worth saying, but both for those who go regularly to church and for those who only make tentative approaches by their use of the Occasional Offices so often it is not the way they experience how they are perceived. More than anything, it is this sense of being valued for who they are that both clergy and laity long for. There is so much in society that militates against such interpersonal relationships, but also the history of the Church is short on conspicuous examples of places where the vision in these verses from Philippians has been a reality. Our hearts warm to the story of St Lawrence, Archdeacon of Rome during the persecution of Valerian and, as such, keeper of the treasures of the Church. When asked by the authorities to produce them, he asked for a day in which to collect them, and spent the time in visiting the poorest quarters of the city. The next day he appeared at the tribunal, taking with him a great crowd of beggars and cripples. 'There are the treasures of the Church,' he said to the presiding magistrate.

This is a far cry from Pope Pius' adage in 1906,

> There are the members of the various orders of the hierarchy and the multitude of believers. The duty of the multitude is to allow themselves to be ruled and to follow obediently the direction of the Office holders.

And, in general, there is a slowly growing appreciation that the future of the Church lies with both priests and people together. Much has been written about the rediscovery of the whole *laos*, and theological colleges put many hours into trying to make this a reality in the minds of future clergy.

There is a new pointer to this mutuality in the rediscovery of the permanent diaconate. While this is more advanced within the Roman Catholic Church, there are signs of it becoming a reality within the Anglican Church too. With the ordination of women has come a small but not insignificant number of men and women who perceive their vocation to be diaconal. To cater for them, the Diaconal Association of the Church of England has been formed, with over a hundred members, and much work and thought is going into trying to define the ministry of a deacon in today's Church. Perhaps the most important facet of all this is a conscious reappraisal of the role of the deacon in the liturgy. Traditionally, the deacon is the one who links the people to the priest at the altar, who symbolizes the bringing of the world by the congregation to lay it before God and his transforming love. Many of the traditional tasks of the deacon are now shared by the laity, but it is the servant task of the whole Church, symbolized by the deacon, to carry in the Gospel and to read it – to be the bearer of the Good News to the people of God, to intercede for the world as its servant, to call the people to peace with one another, to send them out into the world as its servants. This allows the laity to see themselves mirrored not only in the priestly ministry, but also in that of the deacon. Christ is both Priest and Servant in his Church, and this must be reflected both in the priestly intercession of the whole people of God and also in their diaconal service in the world.

It is this latter which illuminates the role of the Church in the world. It is our responsibility to bring the world, as it impinges on each of us, with us to each Eucharist; but also, we have to serve it and to love it as Christ does. When priest and people really believe this, every person feels that their whole life is valued by the congregation, unlike this sales manager:

> I am now a sales manager of a major steel company. In the almost 30 years of my professional career, my church has never once suggested that there should be any type of accounting of my on-the-job ministry to others. My church has never once offered to improve those skills which could make me a better minister, nor has it ever asked if I needed any kind of support in what I am doing.
>
> There was never an enquiry into the types of ethical decisions I must face, or whether I seek to communicate the faith to my co-workers. I have never been in a congregation where there was any type of public affirmation of a ministry in my career. In short I must conclude that my church really doesn't have the least interest whether or how I minister in my daily work.[2]

Instead, there is again a mutuality, a mirroring, between priest and people. It is the vocation of the lay people to serve God in the world. The priestly vocation is not identical, but rather it is so to know the dimensions of the locality and parish, that s/he can not only hold it in their heart, but also be the one who discerns the overall pattern, who can understand the relationship between the different ministries of members of the congregation. This is described by Vincent Donovan in *Christianity Rediscovered*:

> I wanted to know what they would call their priest. They discussed it at length. Two terms which they might have been expected to choose, they rejected out of hand. *Laibon*, witch doctor, and *legwanan*, chief. They wanted to be rid of the *laibon*, their version of the pagan priest. And chief, even though it was a beautiful concept, they felt they had no place for in a Christian community. For the same reason they rejected *olkarsis*, meaning the rich one, powerful one, influential one, and *ol kitok* the head one, the main one, the first. Their playback of the gospel and the response to the gospel saw no need of such dominant characters in the Christian community. Surprisingly to me they did not want to designate their priest as pastor. There were good shepherds and bad shepherds, and any shepherd was concerned with his flock alone, and there were many flocks in the community.
>
> There was one role in the Masai community which appealed very much to them. He was a man present to every community, who was interested in all the flocks of the community and essential to the life of the community and interested in all phases of that life. He was a man to whom anyone could turn for special difficulties and help ... They were called *ilaretok* and represented an extraordinary aspect of pagan life. The word literally means helpers, yet it carried with it all the overtones and connotations of servants. They were helpers or servants of the community ... These new African Christians do not conceive of the priest as preacher, prophet, prayer or sacramentalist. Such a designation would effectively kill the priesthood and at the same time deprive the community as a whole of the power of the sacraments. They rather think of the priest as the one (seemingly the *only* one) who can bring a community into existence, call it together, hold it together, enable the community to function as a community, and enable this community to function as a community, and enable each member to carry out his or her Christian task in the community. Without this *helper* the Christian community can neither exist or function. With him it becomes a eucharistic community with a mission. It will be noted that familiar questions, which are often asked to test the orthodoxy of theories concerning the priesthood, such as whether the community thinks it can hold the Eucharist

or Mass without their priest, are answered in a new and surprising way.[3]

A scenario where the people of God in any one place take seriously the daily setting of each person for their mirroring the diaconal ministry of Christ would be extremely unusual, but also 'missionary' in the best sense. For clergy to expect to learn the details of each person's *Sitz im Leben*, and with them to struggle to determine the ethical, intellectual, servant demands placed upon them would entail listening skills of a very high order, let alone a grasp of ethics and of the interface between the faith and the modern world. Ideally each person needs to see themselves as entrusted by the whole people of God with their ministry in their particular place of work or of daily life, and the intercessions and offering at the Eucharist should reflect this. How many churches pray regularly and methodically for the places in which their members minister/ work? Ideally each person will come to expect the parish priest to elucidate for them and with them their own particular part in a far larger jigsaw, and by prayer, discussion, mutual exploration help them more effectively to live the Christ-life in their particular sphere.

The current shortage of vocations to the ordained ministry can either be seen as a looming disaster for the Church or it can be welcomed for the necessity that it has brought with it for a greater use of the laity in the pastoral work of the parish. It may not be simply coincidence that the greatest strides in the use of the pastoral ministry of the laity have been made in the Roman Catholic Church, whose shortage of clergy is even more dire than in the Church of England. Nonetheless, most dioceses now run schemes for training the laity, and more and more parishes have lay ministers. Perhaps the real test comes in the area of pastoral decision-making, when the priest dares to share in it with the laity whose goodwill and free time the priest desperately needs if the charge given at ordination is to be fulfilled. This does not mean that the laity usurp the role of the priest. The priest is the one whose vocation and whose charge at ordination they mirror. While all of it is held in the priest's person, it is lived out in the life of the congregation, so that those gifts in which the priest is lacking can be found in some of the laity, but any lay ministry is reciprocated in the total calling of the priest.

But laity are no more likely to fulfil their Christian vocations than the clergy unless they learn ways of prayer that allow them to draw deeply on the spiritual resources of the Church. There often seems to be a hidden assumption that it is only the clergy who can or who need to keep up a strict regime of prayer, but the reality is that a surprisingly large number of laity do exactly this. Again, the two vocations may need different ways of prayer but, on the other hand, there may be very little difference to be discerned. Some laity, especially the retired and the housebound, have hidden lives of prayer, which almost exactly mirror that of the priest. But the central issue is not about who prays the most or the best; it is about this same reciprocity, this same mutuality. Again, it is the priest who holds in their person the icon of the Church as pray-er and holds the bishop's authority to administer the sacraments, but none of these has any meaning unless it is echoed by the body, responded to within the body, done in the name of the body. It has to be said that for many laity their parish priest does not bespeak the lifting up of the heart and soul to God. They feel unable to approach such a priest because they see no signs that prayer is the major priority, and they go elsewhere for the medicine of the soul, to retreat houses, religious communities, spiritual directors lay or ordained. There is so often an aching void within the laity, who long for their deep spiritual awareness to be mirrored in the priest. A similar longing is also within those who do not come to church, but go instead to one or other form of folk religion.

As Kenneth Leech makes clear in his recent book *The Sky is Red*,[4] caution has to be exercised in responding to the modern-day emphasis on 'spirituality', and simply to allow it to be the individual's search for 'personal wholeness, inner peace and enhanced consciousness' is not what Christian faith is about. However, taking seriously the responsibility of each individual member of a congregation to see their day-to-day life/work as their sphere of ministry begins to make demands on a person that can be sustained only by a renewed life in Christ. Any community of Christians needs to see as an essential part of their corporate life together the discovery for each person of the appropriate way for them to find the strength they need for their part in the Church's mission. Living the Christian life and living close to God have to go hand in hand. The sense that the priest is the obvious resource for this has often faded, because so many priests are too busy (apparently), or too involved in other things. To suggest to clergy that they might use a season of the Church's year to make appointments with each of their congregation to be available to listen to them and to resource them is rarely met with much enthusiasm. And yet without this intimate knowledge of each person's particular needs it is impossible for clergy to offer potential resources, to make use of so much that is on offer both in dioceses or nationally. In my own experience of 11 years as a diocesan officer concerned with the development and growth of the laity, I was constantly astonished by how parish clergy did not seem to see the relationship between the individual needs of their parishioners and so much information sent out to them month by month. By contrast, those clergy who had a grasp of the needs of each individual found ways to encourage people to take the step to take part in something outside the parish, or else to come together as a congregation often with a facilitator from outside the parish, to discover what should be their next steps together as a whole congregation.

Indeed, the main setting for the growth of the individual should ideally be within the congregation in which he or she find themselves. Tim Gorringe, in his biography of Alan Ecclestone, rightly makes much of his understanding of 'church'. In a chapter aptly titled 'Nurturing the human soul', he quotes Alan's words:

> It is our contention that nothing more important confronts the Church than the task of recovering its essential character of liberating what is God given, of discerning basic truths and enabling it to work like leaven again.[5]

He continues:

> For this task the sermon as a mode of education was clearly quite inadequate. The need was for real questions and discussion, the possibility of tussling out difficult issues. Moreover the agenda could not be set by a lectionary but was, rather, built from concern for what was happening in the contemporary world, what was given in the Christian inheritance and what confronts us as the job of Church people ... The job of the Church is not to help to provide stock answers, but rather to help people to see where they are in the crisis, and to begin asking questions ... They tried to live by Florence Allshorn's motto, 'Never stop asking to be made to see. Seeing is the biggest thing in the world.'[6]

Alan Ecclestone, who served the parish of Darnall in the east end of Sheffield from 1942 to 1970, brought to it from the parish of Sneyd the concept of the parish meeting as the answer to how his vision of life in the body of Christ could be effected. For congregations to be rediscovering the meaning of its 'embodiment of the I-in-You, You in Me relationship which Christ prayed for', there should be two activities each week only to which they were committed, the parish Eucharist and the parish meeting. Shortly after arriving in Darnall, Alan described this:

> The Parish Meeting is simply the calling together of the worshippers, not to be addressed by a speaker, not to be a study group, not to be a 'working group', not to be any of these sectional groups, but to be the Church facing its daily work and ready to find out just how it is to be tackled. Let it be understood that (this assembling) is the other half of the

supreme act of worship and no less vital in our Christian life. We are not experimenting in novelties, but setting out to recover a portion of our Christian heritage which has been mislaid. We are, in fact, tackling the job which underlies or precedes all plans for evangelization ... The aim and value of the Parish Meeting is not to be realized in the passing of resolutions, but in the kind of change of attitude towards the life, work and membership of the Church which it brings.[7]

While the parish meeting may not be the tool for today's Church, it is worth pondering how Alan Ecclestone, nurtured by the Catholic Crusade in his formative years, sought to discover ways in which every single member of a congregation might achieve their full sense of personal self-worth, within the setting of the whole congregation as it grew in love for each other and so for the world. To have this as his aim redefined, almost imperceptibly, his own understanding of priesthood. For him it made sense only within the body of Christ in a given place, as together they wrestled with the week-by-week task of understanding how their life together should impact on the world, as together they grew in their understanding of the complexity of that world.

There is a sense in which any set of essays purporting to describe or encompass the meaning of priesthood, even 'in a people's Church' may well find itself setting out the notion of two standards; two standards of pray-ers, two standards of personal relationships, two standards of witness and of lifestyle. While there may well be a difference in the way in which any standard applies to each particular vocation, to that of priest and laity, it is hard to discern that one is higher than the other. The suggestion in *Issues in Human Sexuality* that there was one greatest good for the clergy and another for the layman cannot hold if there is this sense of reciprocity, of mirroring each other within the life of the Church. 'What is good for the goose, is good for the gander.' If all are in Christ, all partake of his life, all are called to the same imitation of the mind of Christ. To suggest otherwise is immediately to postulate two levels of citizenship of the Kingdom, rather than to see the two vocations as part of a greater whole. In the *Tablet* of 15 August 1998, Bishop Richard Harries describes the conclusion in *Issues in Human Sexuality* as 'respect for the conscientious judgment of those lay people who before God share their lives with someone of the same sex'. Leaving aside the vital issues at stake, to suggest that laity can have one mind and clergy another seems totally to blow apart the interconnectedness, the interdependence, the mirroring of priest and people. In this age of change and of a reassessment of so much that previously seemed to be so clear, the Church may be learning to live within a whole series of dualities of integrities, of contradictory understandings of the faith. If this is the case, then the priest and people desperately need a new understanding of the unity in diversity which is spelt out within the Eucharist, where all equally are included within the total drama of salvation, even though each of them is at a different place on their faith journey. The priest then has to mirror this unity in diversity, to hold in some kind of inner tension in himself the many-faceted jewel that is the people of God in that place, and the priest and laity together have to be so grounded in Christ that their confidence allows for difference.

There can be no other way, given the fact that we no longer live in relatively static communities, where there has been a common lived experience, a common education, a common history. Any community, and therefore any congregation, now contains within itself not only people from all over the British Isles, but people from all over the world. The Church, in as far as it mirrors society, has within any congregation not only cradle Anglicans, but those reared in other Christian traditions, quite apart from those new to faith, let alone to the faith, people touched and moulded by the very heterogeneous society and world in which we now live. It is this polyglot, polymath kind of community that the priest must seek to mirror, and that will learn to live with its own diversity and to rejoice in its difference only if their priest also takes delight in it, and sees its unity to be held within the Eucharist.

So, to return to the image with which this brief essay started – that of a significant drama being played out by an interlocking, by a mutual reflection of actors and of participative audience, where for the full import of the story, both must extend its meaning within and beyond themselves. It could be said that as the third millennium begins, the Anglican Church, and the greater Christian world and Christian history to which we belong, find themselves part of one of the most significant scenes, on which the meaning of the future somehow depends. Often it seems as though we have to exercise that particular description of faith, as 'living in a room without a floor'. There is a sense that none of us knows the way through, none of us has a handle on the future. Rather, to nerve ourselves for the journey, priest and people together need both to draw on the riches and experience of the Church which preceded us, and also all, together, have to learn to find ways to draw on the depths of their own experience, to drink from their own wells, and to offer the crumbs for the feeding of the whole community. The priest may hold the treasures of the Church's wisdom in a special way from the time spent at theological college, but within the experience of the people of God there is a wealth of learning and of lived and inherited experience. The task of today's Church is to discover how all of this may become the ground on which we can safely walk as we move into the future.

PART TWO
THE PRIEST IN RELATIONSHIP

Film stars depend entirely on pleasing others. The priest, however, can exercise real power. Does priesthood lose anything by shunning power games? Is it possible to have the courage to be servants? Strip away the trappings of parish and status, then, to see what is left in a priestly ministry which might be thought marginal ...

5
Simple Gifts: Priesthood in a Praying Community

SISTER BARBARA JUNE SLG

The Church of England rejoices in acronyms and has seemed increasingly tempted to have recourse to the unlovely abbreviated language expressed in capital letters. BCP, ASB, ABM, OLM – numerous examples might be cited, despite the strong challenge now being made by the visually more interesting but no less cryptic logos. Lacking a logo I considered it might have been an acceptable shorthand to entitle this contribution simply PPC, using those letters to stand not for *Priests in a People's Church* but 'Priesthood in a Praying Community'. I need to explain from the start that for me this means being a priest in a monastic community, the Sisters of the Love of God.

In order to explore this theme I have chosen, rather than confronting it head on, to follow Emily Dickinson's dictum and 'tell it slant'. To attempt this I propose to come at it slantwise from two different angles. In the first part I shall use the Shaker hymn 'Simple gifts' as a basis. In two short verses it summarizes with a memorable and remarkable clarity some of what priesthood in a community living under monastic vows bestows and demands. Then, second, I shall myself have recourse to another acronym, the much disputed NSM, and try to show how – when interpreted in a way rather different from usual – it can shed a biblical light on the personal experience of one priest in a praying community.

Simple gifts

First, let us dance with the Shakers! After all, a settled priesthood in a standstill Church is not to be desired now, even if ever it was. A gentle but compelling sense that a Church on the move may want to dance to a different music is the justification for appropriating for use in this rather different context words that were first composed to accompany a dance and to celebrate the total commitment of a community of wholehearted Shaker believers. The tune to which this hymn was originally sung is well known and popular, being the one that Sydney Carter adapted for 'Lord of the dance' and that Aaron Copland orchestrated in 'Appalachian Spring'. The words are these:

'Tis the gift to be simple,
'Tis the gift to be free,
'Tis the gift to come down where we ought to be.
And when we find ourselves in the place just right
'Twill be in the valley of love and delight.

When true simplicity is gained
To bow and to bend we shan't be ashamed.
To turn, turn, will be all our delight
Till by turning, turning, we come round right.[1]

Many scholarly exponents of Christian priesthood and of contemplative community life have laboured to formulate and express its meaning in words, with much less success and immediacy. It takes a childlike delight in the surprisingness of things as they are to reach out a hand to grasp at a sunbeam or a jet of water and to laugh at the elemental elusiveness of both; they won't be caught and held – gleaming and dancing things that they are. So too priesthood in a praying community finds expression not in words on a page, but in a song in the heart.

So what has this hymn to tell us about being a priest living under the traditional vows of a monastic community? First and most important of all, that as for every Christian this union with God through Christ is all *gift*. As with the threefold gift of creation, redemption and sanctification, the traditional vows of poverty, chastity and obedience belong inextricably together and belong too with the gifted calling to be a priest. This multifaceted three-dimensional gift is bigger than the recipient, bigger than the heart can hold, 'pressed down, shaken together and running over', a bounty that won't be caught and held, and yet can catch and hold us and carry us in a tide of dancing sunlight to where we belong to be.

The title of the hymn, 'Simple gifts', emphasizes this gifted aspect of priestly ministry. 'Vocation' is primarily a given calling rather than a subjective choice. As Christians our union with God is something given to grow in us; something into which we ourselves grow from baptism onwards; something by which we grow into ourselves or, more precisely, something by which we grow into the measure of the stature of the fullness of Christ. From this perspective, vows of whatever kind are best seen essentially as gifts rather than as promises we make. Priesthood in community is something to be accepted and unwrapped, so to say, rather than something to be achieved, done or performed. Moreover, all vows are gifts in both senses of that word. They are birthday presents and also hidden talents; they have to be unwrapped but also developed and employed.

The hymn specifies that the gifts are three:

'Tis the gift to be simple,
'Tis the gift to be free,
'Tis the gift to come down where we ought to be.

Can these three 'simple gifts' really be applied to a life lived under monastic vows and to the life of a priest? They seem to me to harmonize remarkably well with both. Let us consider each gift in turn and explore the correspondence first with each of the traditional vows and then with the no-less-committed life of a priest. It is a precise and subtle harmony and correspondence, which depends on matching each of the simple gifts to all three monastic vows in turn, not pairing them off.

The 'gift to be simple' accords with the vow of poverty in one way, with chastity in another, and with obedience in a third way. To elaborate a little on that statement: poverty is the 'gift to be simple' in the sense that it means a simple and entire dependence on Christ – 'as having nothing and yet possessing all things'. It sounds simple enough, but there is nothing easy about it! Chastity is 'the gift to be simple' in another way. It means having the whole being set on God. What could be simpler than that? The words convey something of the passionate singleness of heart that total commitment to God in a life of prayer demands and bestows. Obedience too is 'the gift to be simple'. It means a constant simple 'Yes', a synergy of will with God, utterly simple, 'costing not less than everything'.

For a priest, the 'gift to be simple' may or may not be able to express itself in a simple lifestyle, very probably not in our Western affluent and complex culture. Here and now we are more often paralysingly conscious of the absence of simplicity rather than of its presence. It seems crowded out by clutter, double-mindedness and obfuscating complications. But, what is it about, after all? Not about 'the simple life' but being single-hearted in the quest for God and irrevocably committed. The nature of the commitment made publicly at ordination can make subsequent decisions and choices simpler – not easier but sharper. The overlap and fusion of two similar but also subtly different perceptions of 'the gift to be simple' is experienced by a priest in a monastic community in a very real and particular way.

The 'gift to be free' pertains to all three vows in the same kind of way. Poverty can enable absolute positive freedom from every kind of obsessive selfish possessiveness or ownership. For every Christian and peculiarly for every priest the 'gift to be free' is to be part of 'the Lord's thing' – *Kyriakon*, the Church – and to be no longer solely self-possessed. This freedom is expressed in the opening words of the Methodist Covenant Prayer – 'I am no longer my own but thine.' Chastity too is the 'gift to be free', the paradox of free love pushed to its limits. Even more paradoxically, obedience is the vow of freedom. To obey is a free response of love.

The 'gift to be free' is about choice and the freedom to choose in love. It is a risky and rough-edged gift. There is nothing smooth or automatic about it. For the priest there is a gritty deposit of paradox that cannot be sieved out. The God who asks for obedience is the one 'whose service is perfect freedom'; the one whom John Donne addresses with the claim 'I, except thou enthral me, never can be free.' A German Lutheran Sister speaks with disarming mispronunciation of the three *wows*. Obedience – WOW!

The 'gift to be free' – but free from what and free for what? Confronting those questions as we are loosed and let go free is to stand with Lazarus new stumbling into the sunlight.

The 'gift to come down where we ought to be' is about finding our place, about humbly coming home. The adverb 'down' hints at poverty of status as well as true subordination in mutual obedience. The clause 'where we ought to be' describes our proper place, our right environment, our native land, our own true soil where we can flourish and abound, rooted and grounded in love. However much 'where we ought to be' involves searching and journeying, we recognize the place when we come there, when we come down upon it. The priest, the nun, the husband or wife, anyone who has dared to make a life commitment can say somehow and sometimes, 'This is it.' This ultimate sense of being where we belong to be is taken up and expanded in the next two lines of the hymn:

> *And when we find ourselves in the place just right*
> *'Twill be in the valley of love and delight.*

It may seem to be pushing the bounds of credibility too far to apply these words literally to the territory and environs of monastic or priestly life. Yet all the same they ring true as a description of the place of vocation. It is a place where most commonly we are surprised to find ourselves to be. Vocationally the 'place just right' may be scenically uninspiring, rackety and begrimed. The monastic buildings may be draughty and ill lit; the parish church may be musty and incongruous but, still with a sense that we are where we belong to be, they are for us part of the 'place just right' and, despite all appearances to the contrary, 'the valley of love and delight'. That is a very real gift in a world and time when belongingness at many levels has given way to a profound and devastating sense of alienation.

Of course the three 'simple gifts' are not exclusively bestowed on those who have made the vowed commitment that has been described so far. We need only think of Bunyan's shepherd boy singing in the Valley of Humiliation as a prototype of the simple believer. His song corresponds wonderfully with 'Simple gifts'. Being simple, free and in our right place are gifts properly part of every Christian's baptismal endowment. Discovering 'where we ought to be' is about developing our baptismal identity, the 'who we are to be'. Each and every vocation can experience something of the humility of 'coming down' and the standing sure-footed in the 'place just right'. It may be that the recognition of them is just easier for those who have the chance to live enclosed within the stability of community life.

The last verse of the hymn is about submission and conversion:

When true simplicity is gained
To bow and to bend we shan't be ashamed.
To turn, turn, will be all our delight
Till by turning, turning, we come round right.

Submission, conversion, metanoia, repentance – these, like simplicity, are 'gained'. That is to say, they are hard won. They are certainly not dispositions that any Christian, and therefore any priest or religious, can automatically and painlessly claim. Gaining them asks of us cooperation, willing assent, a searching response. True simplicity and being able to bow and bend without shame are the fruits of what Bonhoeffer would call 'costly grace'. Community life gives infinite scope for bowing and bending in a kind of ring dance of reciprocal obedience and submission. A priest too may expect to be presented with daily opportunities to reverence and assent to the demands or commands or requests of others. Bowing and bending are not just priestly movements in a liturgical context. They keep the soul supple!

'To turn, turn will be all our delight …' Notice that this turning is an oft-repeated action, and one every Christian constantly needs to engage in. It begins with that decisive, once-for-all first step we are asked to take in baptism. 'Do you turn to Christ?' 'I turn to Christ.' The initiative for turning, for conversion, seems to lie with us and we must act. But equally the ability to turn is a response to an initiative beyond us that has been already taken. It is a yielding, if you like, to the gravitational pull of redemption.

It is worth reflecting a bit more generally on the place of conversion both in general and in the particular context of monastic priesthood. Conversion for the young and those at the start of their Christian pilgrimage may mean a radical and visible change of lifestyle. But the work of 'turning, turning' in middle age and onward is no less remarkable and creative, though it is likely to be more hidden and less spectacular. Conversion is a mystery of transfiguration and new creation open to us here and now, but with an eternal dimension to it. This is the conversion envisaged when we think about the changing of 'our vile body that it may be fashioned like unto his glorious body' (Phil. 3.21, AV) or when we speak in terms of putting on 'the new man which is being renewed in knowledge after the image of him that created him' (Col. 3.10, AV). For a priest, how this 'turning, turning' of conversion – being changed beyond all recognition – can be brought about in each unique here and now is a question we may ask ourselves and ask God in prayer. It is a leading question and it may lead us into some pretty uncomfortable places. But those who risk asking the question may discover that the answer has already been given to us in our baptismal commitment and has been renewed with fresh affirmation in our ordination vows or those of our religious profession or both. By 'turning, turning' every moment, in each unpromising situation, with each ordinary routine demand, we 'come round right'.

We turn and we return, for to turn is to turn again, to return. This is the basic figure in the intricately simple ring dance that is our Christian life. St Maximus the Confessor celebrates the 'turning, turning' in a letter written some 12 centuries earlier than the Shaker hymn.

> The heralds of the truth and ministers of divine grace who have explained to us from the beginning right down to our own time each in our own day the saving will of God, say that nothing is so dear and loved by him as when people turn to him with true repentance. (Letter 11)[2]

One step round and the prodigal's return has begun. The homecoming is celebrated with music and dancing, and in the warmth of the father's embrace he knows that he has 'come round right'. One last step round and each recipient of the 'simple gifts' will turn to face the Giver of them all, and no words will be needed in the joy of that recognition, when we shall be like him, for 'we shall see him as he is' (1 John 3.2, AV).

Nazareth-style ministry

'I turn to Christ.' This can take us into the second slantwise way of considering priesthood in a praying community. I was first led to think about this aspect when I heard the acronym NSM, which usually stands for non-stipendiary ministry, given a novel interpretation when it was applied to a colleague in the parish where I trained. 'Do you know what the letters NSM after Angela's name mean?' I heard the congregation being asked. 'Those letters stand for "Nazareth-style ministry".' I asked myself what it might also mean to define the ministry of monastic or contemplative priesthood in those terms. By looking at some examples I hope to illustrate my conclusion that it is an appropriate acronym.

'I turn to Christ.' Nazareth-style ministry has primarily to be learned and exercised by turning to Jesus of Nazareth. Of course it is only one style among many complementary and needful Christian ministries both lay and ordained; for if the model for all is Jesus Christ, our great High Priest, the scope is wide indeed. Ordinarily, and for obvious reasons, the active and pastoral side of priestly ministry finds its inspiration in turning to Christ as Teacher, Healer and Shepherd; and the priest at prayer looks to Christ crucified or to the ascended Lord forever interceding in the heavens. So what is properly the nature and scope of this Nazareth-style ministry?

First of all it is located in the place of annunciation. As with every vocation one is called to it, sometimes totally unexpectedly, perhaps in some unguarded moment. Moreover, it happens in a place that does not seem to have much going for it or to arouse great expectations. 'Can anything good come out of Nazareth?' There are both positive and negative aspects to this kind of ministry that accord with the experience of Jesus in his home town, so to say. Let us look at some of them, recognizing from the start that they cannot be neatly subdivided into either 'positive and good' or 'negative and bad'. They belong together and, as the Japanese proverb wisely says, 'The opposite side has its opposite side.'

That said, there are many positive and good things about priesthood in a praying community that belong with concepts like hiddenness, ordinariness and being nothing special. I used at one time to think that being ordained within a community such as mine, whose main work is prayer, was more like being a worker priest than anything else, and jokingly I sometimes adapted the acronym MSE to MNSE and described myself as a minister in non-secular employment! Plainly the worker-priest concept is not alien to the hidden, ordinary life of Jesus at Nazareth. Being a priest in a praying community demands and bestows a certain double hiddenness. On the one hand there is the general hidden nature of the community itself, a community whose life has nothing to show for it, and then there is also the particular personal hiddenness within that. Outwardly and visibly there is nothing in my community to distinguish a priest sister from any other; all wear look-alike habits. 'I shall wear *nothing* to distinguish me from my sisters' as the joke goes!

Then the pattern of the life and the routine of the days have a good lot of ordinariness about them. That is an unqualified blessing. A shared place, shared meals, shared work, shared worship – these are features we have in common with that settled Nazareth-style populace. The chapel focuses our common worship in the same way as the synagogue did theirs. Like them we are able to say the psalms day in day out together and to hear the Scriptures amid fellow believers rather than alone. This is in contrast to the somewhat more isolated and irregular opportunity for common prayer some priests have, and it is a great bonus and support. At the same time there is the inescapable element of aloneness that I take to be a dimension in the life of every priest. The 'collaborative ministry' of a monastic community essentially includes this no less than the collaborative ministry of the carpenter's shop.

Importantly, a priest in community is in some way a 'minister without portfolio'. Plainly a Nazareth-style minister has not to undertake tasks of leadership in the way that one with the care of a parish is obliged to do. This is not at all an 'up-front' role. There is no career structure, and no aspirations towards ecclesiastical preferment. While this fact can be recognized and appreciated as another kind of 'gift to be free', at times it would be easier if it were a job with 'something to show for it' and a distinguishable job description. It is easy to do nothing when there is nothing to do! Yet, as far as leadership goes, the non-eventful lifestyle of Jesus himself at Nazareth surely differed in many ways from what was to follow after his baptism, beginning in Galilee.

The mission of a priest called to 'Galilee-style ministry' is an active one. Ordination for the majority may lead to new territory and a considerable change of lifestyle. My own experience by contrast has been and is very different. No outward and visible upheaval, no moving house to a new place, no new circumstances. There is an element of all this of course for any priest who stays put after ordination and has an ongoing family life and perhaps some other professional work. During my training I had the dual experience of presiding at the Eucharist in the parish occasionally and also sometimes in our convent chapel. It was instructive to discover the difference between doing this in church amid a congregation that by and large only knew me in that context, and here on home ground where I am and remain uncomfortably and belongingly well known in a much more personal way. Married priests must share an experience something like this when the family comes to church. There is something to be said for having a chance to begin as priest in new pastures. It is difficult to be a butterfly where one has been a caterpillar!

However, Nazareth-style ministry is profoundly and precisely about being well known and no stranger. That can bring its own sense of scandal. 'Where did this man get all this? Is not this the carpenter's son?' Again, I am well aware that there must at times be an element of rejection in every priest's experience. This can be simply part of how it is. However, there is something over and above all this. Alongside the non-acceptance that familiarity can provoke there is the helplessness engendered by unbelief. This is vividly and poignantly revealed in the gospel accounts of the hostility the people of Nazareth felt towards Jesus on his return. His being powerless in the face of their unbelief is a constant reminder that, however much we as priests may want to do, the outcome lies outside our control or determination. Yet this acceptance of being disempowered, disabled, helpless is very much the stuff of monastic life and contemplative intercession. It may be a hard-won willed passivity, but nonetheless a first fruits of what in my community we call 'the love behind the Passion'. The author of the letter to the Hebrews clearly distinguishes the suffering, sacrificial priesthood of Jesus from the Levitical priesthood.

It would be misleading to give the impression that, because Nazareth-style ministry is more about continuity than contrast, ordination has made no difference to me or to the community. Personally I have always believed that being a nun and a priest is much more like wife'n mother than fish'n chips! There is a fusion of vocation and no conflict of identity. But ordination does make an irrevocable difference. There is a 'before' and 'after' and a conviction that something has happened that cannot be unhappened. At a personal level I have felt that during these past few years part of the grace of office has been the abiding sense that because there was no precedent or obvious role model within my community, the Sisters of the Love of God, I need in a new way to depend wholly on God, Father, Son and Holy Spirit. At the deepest level that has been peace-making. Monastic priesthood is at least as much to do with the life of the cell as with life in the sanctuary. Here within enclosure, the pastoral elements in every priestly ministry are exercised by us all in different ways and at different times – through our intercessory prayer, through our hospitality and welcome, through our listening to and travelling spiritually alongside those who come seeking that kind of ministry, and most of all through our serving Christ in one another and loving as he loves us. It is hard to explain, but I believe that our monastic life is a ministry of presence and recognition of the 'in stillness nailed' prayer of Jesus Christ, our great High Priest. In some indefinable but nonetheless real way ordination has enabled something to become outward and visible that for me was there inwardly and spiritually from the start, and which has perhaps been implicit in our vocation as Sisters of the Love of God.

Much of what I have tried to 'tell slant' in these pages necessarily reads like a peculiarly personal testimony. I have also been very conscious of being very near the beginning of this Nazareth-style ministry received alongside and within the simple gifts of life under the vows of poverty, chastity and obedience. But my hope is that as this new millennium unfolds the bounds of ministerial priesthood may be extended, as they have already begun to be, to encompass all kinds of new possibilities. There have always been and long may there continue to be priests where the people's Church is. May we also be able to go on being bold enough to cross thresholds and frontiers to rediscover the Church where the priest is.

When it is working healthily, monastic life sets a model of community as *co-inherence*, an inhering in each other where us-and-them attitudes become impossible to sustain. This is a central 'mystery' of priestly ministry: being a person who 'feels with' the other, and looks on the sinner's outward behaviour, however bad it may sometimes be, with understanding from within.

But how may the one who is this kind of attentive servant yet be able to speak with authority? ...

6
Priest and Victim

GEORGE GUIVER CR

A popular way to cope with problems is to blame other people, something in fact we rely on in order to stay at peace with ourselves. This varies from person to person and community to community, but blame is alive and well in all of us. If the post arrives late we complain about the post; a train seat is double-booked and we blame the ticket-collector; if the economy goes into decline we blame the government; public facilities are vandalized and we blame the youngsters. If our new radio stops working we take it back and play merry hell. Shop assistants, receptionists and other 'front people' of large institutions frequently bear the brunt of our blame.

In a stationer's shop on a hot summer's day a man shouts with anger at a young girl behind the counter. The ink in his new ballpoint pen has melted and made a sticky mess in the inside pocket of his jacket, and a nasty stain on the lining. The girl tries to explain that it is not a good idea to keep ballpoint pens in inside pockets in warm weather, but is unable to add 'particularly if you are overweight and hot anyway'. He becomes aggressive, even though nothing can be achieved by putting her through this ordeal – she hasn't made the pen, she has enough personal problems of her own at the moment without all this, and both she and he know that if anyone other than the owner is to blame, it is the manufacturer. She knows she can't exchange it, but can only advise the man to write to the makers. He, however, cannot see the difference between girl and manufacturer. They are all one thing, 'thing' being the operative word. This is not a vulnerable human being in front of him but an official, faceless representative of the villain of the piece. He turns to the people in the queue for support, urging his case with righteous disgust – the rightness of his case self-evident. In attempting to forge a unity with others against the girl, he angrily masks the conflict within himself.

Looking at the pale and shaken assistant, who as it happens has just been jilted by her boyfriend and also has 'flu coming on, we can reflect on the lot of innocent people, little people, we might say in a gospel sense, who find themselves at the public interface of large institutions. In the same way, the public life of our society often works on a basis of blaming victims. If serious irregularities are found in a social services department, the head, even if her own conduct has been exemplary, must resign, providing the necessary visible victim. Often in such institutions misinformation and gossip can make people entrenched in their caricature of the person being blamed. The like-minded talk together and stoke each other up in their one-sided view. If among all the increasingly expensive wonders of modern medical science the public expectation of the health service cannot be met through shortage of cash, hard choices of life and death have to be made, bringing down on the hospital a storm of indictment and protest. A woman loses a baby because she and her family had failed to heed warnings that she was overeating, and in the local paper the family blame the hard-pressed doctors, threatening legal action. Blame is part of child-rearing, of courtship, marriage, of the workplace, and of all the rest of life, and always has been. It is a standard reaction in children, who will regularly blame their brother, sister or playmates when reproved by adults. That is how we start, and that is how we carry on.

The age of the victim

In modern times attitudes have begun to develop away from this culture of blame. There is creeping change, a dawning realization of the predicament of the victim. In eighteenth-century Britain, youngsters could be executed for stealing. Nowadays some people at least are beginning to realize the economic and social factors in the incidence of crime, something clearly demonstrated by statistics. Deprivation, failures in education, lack of secure family life and resulting lack of self-worth are some of the factors now recognized to increase the possibility of criminal behaviour. This awareness has not yet reached all the politicians, nor all of the general public, but an insight that was rare in the eighteenth or even nineteenth centuries is now in circulation. This insight radically changes the mechanics of blame and victimization, often turning it on its head. Now we have access to a new knowledge: we are involved in a shared complicity. Wayne, Mark and Darren steal cars and beat up old people, and while they are responsible for those actions because of their God-given freedom and their own sinfulness, I too am responsible through my passive, uncritical support of a society which has given them terrible home lives and no prospect of a job. The blame now falls on all of us. Had I grown up in Wayne's situation rather than the one I did grow up in, there is a stronger likelihood that I would have behaved in the same way. If I refuse to recognize that, then I am like the Pharisees who said, 'If we had lived in the days of our fathers, we would not have taken part with them in shedding the blood of the prophets' (Matt. 23.30, RSV), when there is every likelihood that they would have done.

This realization is part of something wider, a realization like scales falling from our eyes, insights that have been tellingly depicted by René Girard, especially in his book *Things Hidden Since the Foundation of the World*.[1] Never before has there been so much concern for the victim, for the marginalized, for tolerance of others, and for trying to empathize with the experience of those who suffer. Something new is happening and spreading. Sometimes it tips over into the opposite extreme, a naive idealizing of the sufferer or the marginalized, with a blind spot for any idea that they are also sinful. This naivety only ends by being exploited. The worst thing you can do when faced with a mugger is to try to be nice to him. The indications are that we are gradually learning these lessons, and in the long term the prospect is of a society that will take greater and greater care to be aware of the situation of those who suffer or are disabled or disadvantaged in any way, in a growing awareness of the obvious fact that every person is a sensitive human being.

This attitude of love towards our neighbour is nothing new of course – in the particularly strong form appearing nowadays it was first proclaimed 2,000 years ago by Jesus. Since then Christianity has on the whole made a poor job of living it out. If we look at the way criminals have been treated in Christian societies, or Jews, or women, or the victims of war, we find that for a large part of its history the Church has lived the gospel in an Old-Testament way. Blame, retribution, punishment have had a free rein by and large. Victimization, lording it over people, and the resolution of conflict through violence and the exacting of 'just' penalties have been routine. At the beginnings of Christianity the conditions were set up for the truth about blame to be unmasked, but the process of realizing the full implications has so far taken 2,000 years, and still has a long way to go. The conditions that were set up were the Church with its sacramental order, carrying with it the Scriptures and traditions of the New Way that Jesus ushered in. The realization of the fruits has been slow and gradual. The respect for all, especially the disadvantaged, which is now appearing everywhere, could only come into its own by a gradual process. Through all those centuries it was embodied in the saints here and there, the loving sacrifice of a nurse or nun, the kindliness of an exceptional official, the gentle monarch, the rare priest and even rarer bishop. Even though on the whole Christians have been slow at passing from the Old Testament to the New, the thread of the true gospel appears in people in various places all through Christian history, and can sometimes be seen with a blazing clarity that impresses people of any age. We find an instance in the golden age of the desert fathers and mothers of Egypt, whose wisdom could say, 'A dog is better than I am, for he has love and he does not judge.'[2] As well as storing up ripe wise sayings, these earthy Christians were given to telling stories such as this one:

A brother at Scetis committed a fault. A council was called to which Abba Moses was invited, but he refused to go to it. Then the priest sent someone to say to him, 'Come, for everyone is waiting for you.' So he got up and went. He took a leaking jug, filled it with water and carried it with him. The others came out to meet him and said to him, 'What is this, Father?' The old man said to them, 'My sins run out behind me, and I do not see them, and today I am coming to judge the errors of another.' When they heard that they said no more to the brother but forgave him.[3]

This rejection of victim-hunting runs like a subversive contrary thread among the many failures of Christian history, a thread of lives which by the grace of God have been holy lives, often lived on the margins of the Church.

Violent methods

If the world is now beginning to learn to respect all human beings, whatever their situation, there is, however, still something wrong with this respect – it is undermined, says René Girard, by failure to break out of the victimage process. Much if not all of our struggle for justice, tolerance and freedom is crippled by our use of the very mechanics of blame that cause the problem in the first place. Movements abound for humanitarian ends, but very often they operate by blaming those who do not see things in the same way; they use the same violence – as the man protesting about his pen used violence on the shop assistant, so movements defending victims in fact use violence to achieve their ends: violent language against others, and sometimes violent behaviour. In this way the 'blamers' and the victims mirror each other. Each is a replica of the other; violence begets violence. There are some warnings in the Gospels against those who seek to bring in the kingdom by violent means, especially an ambiguous and haunting saying in Luke: 'The law and the prophets were until John; since then the good news of the kingdom of God is preached, and every one enters it violently' (Luke 16.16, RSV). We instinctively need victims, and cannot see how good can be achieved without the violent use of blame. If we can't do this in defence of victims, you might say, then what on earth can we do? Simply allow the injustice to continue? Christ implies that if justice is obtained by these means, it will not bring peace but will continue the cycle of violence. 'Judge not, that you be not judged.' What are the victims to do then? Are they simply to turn the other cheek for another few millennia?

The problem is compounded by another layer in this new form of victimization: a fashion for making a meal of being a victim. The steady rise in cases of litigation – over unsuccessful medical treatment, contested examination marks, damage caused by falling cutlery in a restaurant – is not only fired by financial considerations, but also by quickness to become a victim and apportion blame. People who used to write to the local paper to complain about something and sign, 'Disgusted', now have a far ampler field for setting other people up on pedestals in order to throw things at them. The mentality of the victim is eating into our soul. Mishaps which once upon a time could be attributed to bad luck or mere frailty or lack of care are now material for the search for someone to blame.

> A victim can be anyone at all with a claim to sympathy, even if he or she has not been hurt directly – and even if he has brought the damage on himself. By this token almost everyone can find something they are a victim of. And, being a victim, they can claim that they are not responsible for what they do ... A man who leans over the stove as he lights the gas, and is burned, sues the gas company.[4]

The parents of Matthew Eappen who died in mysterious, and probably accidental, circumstances at the hands of a young au pair girl in the USA made a dramatic display of their status as victim, and demanded the exacting of a full revenge. They in turn were blamed for taking advantage of a young, inexperienced foreigner; the justice system was blamed for its conduct of the case; the British public was blamed for blaming Americans; and there started up a roundabout of reciprocal blame in which self-proclaimed victims sought their own victims. None of the participants seemed able to see that the justice that they sincerely sought was so overshadowed by the methods of retributive victimization that it would continue to elude them. Victims and victimizers are in fact linked in an unholy alliance – they make a symmetrical double, mirroring each other in exacting eye for eye and tooth for tooth. While ours is very much an age of the victim, it does not yet show much sign of becoming an age which rejects the methods of victimization.

Every reader will be aware that here we have a problem: those who find themselves as victims have a right and even duty to seek justice. Mere compliance with bad behaviour in others can simply amount to collusion: there are moments when a stand has to be made, when wrong has to be exposed and those responsible have to be named. It may even be necessary to persist, in the face of strong resistance, which is of course what Jesus did. Such action is always ambiguous because of our own sin, but the vital point here is that it be done without any vindictiveness or spirit of judgement in the heart (even if it may look like that to those criticized), and with a desire for the good of the one who is opposed. In any quest for truth there must be no quest for victims.

Blame and the priest

The priest is called to be a representative of that strand in Christianity which has moved from the Old Testament to its fulfilment in the New. One distinguishing mark is a habit of seeking to understand the sinner and refusing to sit in judgement. Other people can be irritated by this apparent softness. Some teenagers keep coming into church and larking around. The churchwardens want to take strong measures against them; the priest wants to gain their confidence, to see what can be done. A drug addict is often in the church porch – some congregations may be sympathetic, but in others there may be people who want to show him he is not welcome; even if no one else does, the priest needs to take seriously the predicament the man is in. Religious communities and monasteries are not infrequently asked to offer a temporary home to persons awaiting formal charge or trial for offences of one kind or another. If such guests come to stay, they will receive a warm welcome because the monks and nuns are fully aware of their own share in our corporate sin. This approach is no monopoly of clergy or religious communities, but part of their calling is to represent such a refusal to blame, however well or not it may be represented in the rest of the Church.

The priest is called to have a 'pastoral heart' which knows how to be hardheaded and sensible, while refusing to victimize or let anyone's crime lead us to think we are above their behaviour. The priest's is a delicate balancing act: compassion and empathy have to be paramount, but also the ability to speak with authority, either to the victim or to the victimizers. This needs particularly to be borne in mind where there may be a temptation to be beguiled into being a 'soft touch', in a way which colludes with the sin in the other and makes the situation worse. There can be no guidelines set out in print – you need to develop a feel for it, and be ready to recognize your inability to judge rightly. Always ask, 'Who is the pilot in this situation?' Is it just me, or is it Christ?

Imitation of Christ?

Taking Christ as our model is no straightforward matter. It has long been assumed in Western Christianity that we are called to imitation of Christ. Such imitation, however, fails to take adequate account of our feeble brains, inadequate morals, and unrecognized biases towards fulfilling personal desires. Our capacity for choosing what to imitate is so corrupted that simple talk of 'imitation of Christ' can only be a chimera. The way of Christ can be spoken about and identified, but cannot be copied or reproduced by us. Only Christ can imitate himself in us – we have to put him on, through Christ living the life of Christ in us. How is that to come about?

If the priest wishes to be like Christ, imitation will be an element in the quest for that, but higher than imitation is the work of Christ himself in us, so that the imitating is done not by us alone, but by Christ, Christ taking up his home in us; and one essential condition for that is life in the body of Christ, with our sisters and brothers with whom we are sinners together.

Participation in Christ

The door now opens on another arena. The message about blame, which is a central part of René Girard's philosophy, on which I have relied heavily in this chapter, is echoed in the liturgical theology of the German liturgist Odo Casel, which centres around the word 'Mystery' as used in the New Testament.[5] This Mystery is in fact the 'better way' we have been identifying, but Casel approaches it from another angle, not of imitation but of participation. Like Girard he too points out that this Mystery is a truth after which all the religions have striven, and which came most to the fore in Judaism, but had to wait until Christ for its full revelation. It is the 'Mystery hidden for ages but now made manifest'. This 'Mystery hidden since the foundation of the world' unveils and discredits the vindictive ways of humanity through the saving events recounted in the Gospels. The Mystery is Christ, incarnate, living, dying, rising again. All of the saving events are an incarnation and enfleshing of the 'better way' in which God himself participates and is the central character and victim.

When people encountered Christ in the villages and towns of Palestine, when they were involved in his crucifixion, when they were swept off their feet by the rising of One who was dead, they were seeing, touching, feeling, smelling the Mystery with all their senses. They were participating. To live fully as a human being of flesh and blood is to participate. They had a need to meet the person, and they met him. It was essential to be able to do so. 'He went up into the hills and sat down there. And great crowds came to him' (Matt. 15.29, RSV). If Jesus had simply sent a photograph of himself, or people had just read about him in a personal testimonial, the gospel would have grabbed no one. People needed to meet him, see him, touch him, to be present at the event. It can therefore be no surprise that one of the truly revolutionary aspects of Christianity is the incarnation. There is no substitute for personal flesh-and-blood contact. If they needed to meet him, we do too. Our need is no less than theirs. If they needed the incarnation, then we need the incarnation. That is why we have been made into a people of God, living stones.

When we celebrate the liturgy today we participate in Christ fully in the same way; we participate, put him on; we are enabled to welcome him in, so that he might 'imitate himself' in us, that we might become holy people, people who will shun all vindictiveness against brothers and sisters, who will see what is going on in the temptation to apportion blame and seek recompense. What we see, hear, smell and bump up against in church on a Sunday morning is the living Mystery. We meet Christ just as they did, in these physical events now unfolding in this place of worship. Just as they met him in Galilee, we meet him in the worshipping assembly. Just as they saw and touched and smelt, swimming in the living event, so do we now. Worship is a kind of translation of the saving events. The service brings to us all that was available to them in Palestine.

Blame, the Mystery and the priest

One of the characters in the liturgical drama is the priest. The priest is called to be an apostle and sign of the Mystery, a person in whom this 'better way' can be seen at work. This can come about not through mere imitation, but through participation, by a life of prayer based on repentance, love of neighbour and incorporation in the body of Christ: a thoroughgoing and vigorous participation that affects the whole person.

One of the places where it is clear that the priest is set apart for a purpose is the ministry of absolution. The priest has authority to hear the frankest and most personal outpourings of another person, and then to pronounce in God's name the Good News that their sin is put away for ever. This ministry of reconciliation is for the priest a school in the Mystery of the God in whom there is no blame, in a compassion and generosity which reject any seeking of victims or sitting in judgement. This Good News has lain hidden among us since the foundation of the world, glimpsed here and there in outstanding people, but only fully manifest in Christ.

It is perhaps in the daily recitation of the psalms that the priest is most deluged, sometimes in almost insupportable torrents, with the anguish of a nation which for most of its history had the experience of being a victim. In cries for revenge and retribution, pleas for mercy and for peace, the priest hears again in the context of the Mystery of Jesus Christ voices heard every day in people all around. In the deep, seemingly ineradicable reaction of blaming the other, the psalms lead us in other people's footsteps, treading the way of blame, but all mixed up higgledy-piggledy with insights into divine generosity, in which it is still possible to say 'Blessed be the Lord.'

All acts of worship have this character to some extent, but the Eucharist most of all. When the people of God gather together, fulfilling their various gifts and roles, they are Mystery. The word 'mystery', as well as referring to Christ himself, also means 'sacrament'. The people of God at worship – that is, priest and people together – are a sacrament of the presence of Christ. We each fulfil our role, perhaps giving out books, perhaps singing in the choir, perhaps in the congregation, singing and speaking our part. What we are tempted to do is look for God *behind* the external things of worship, which are seen as some sort of visual aid. The beautiful church, candles, the robes, the pictures. Or, if there are none of these things, the beauty of the simplicity. We take it that they are there to stir us to an inner experience of God. That is the great and age-old mistake of Western Christianity. What we need to realize is that the people we see and shake hands with are that presence of God. The candles and the robes and the music are not simply visual aids, they are, by being used in the body of Christ, the very presence themselves. And at the centre of it the giving of thanks over the bread and wine and their sharing out are in themselves the very presence of the Mystery. We encounter Christ just as closely as anyone in a village in first-century Galilee, and just as physically. We encounter his victimization on the cross, and his vindication.

The life together of Christians, and their worship as one body, are the only ways that the 'better way' can be fully set free in the world. The respect for human beings that we are now seeing coming to birth in our secular society was implanted there by the gospel, and has in due course started to come to fruition through centuries of walking with God in prayer and worship, exposure to the Scriptures, and the witness of outstanding Christians. The best way Christians can make their contribution to this unmasking of the mechanics of victimization is by staying close to those events through which it was originally unmasked, and to the person at the centre of them, Christ the humble servant and cheek-turning victim. This outshines any attempts at imitation that rely solely on ourselves.

The victim and the priest

Every priest will know the experience of being a victim, and will know the strong temptation to boomerang it back on the perpetrator. In every Christian community there are circular dynamics of blame. This is certainly true of the world in which the Church is set. In these circumstances every priest has to be a person who is beginning to get beyond that, a person who recognizes an identity with the wrongdoer. This is one of the characteristic marks of the pastoral mind – it can be maddening to others, who will interpret it as softness, but it is not to be confused with softness. It is an ability, despite whatever a person has done, to know that I myself am also a sinner, and it is an ability to go on from that to seek their good. And even when the priest does have to speak out and protest at the doings of others, it must always be with prayer for them, and the desire for their good. Only this is capable of giving the largeness which

will so change our attitudes to people that we will end up with no patri-
otisms or ideals that divide, not even for the Church. The Church has no
monopoly on the 'more excellent way', but has the gifts, if it will use
them, to go out and water the seeds of that way which are scattered about
in all the world.

High ideals, but frail earthen vessels. How can we live worthily of the gospel, and yet live as the real human beings that we are? In the priest's more intimate relationships this tension can feel particularly sharp ...

7
Marriage, Priesthood and Ministry: Four Vignettes

NICHOLAS AND CHRISTINE HENSHALL

A holy mystery

Andrew and Dawn move together to the table near the altar. On the table stands an icon – the Holy Trinity. And in front of it three candles. Two already burning, the third unlit. Slowly each takes a burning candle and lights the third together.

In our small Christian community weddings are rare. In a good year we will celebrate three. Perhaps because they are infrequent I have come to value them deeply, to delight in being there. And it is always this moment – the lighting of the candle – that delights and draws me most. Watching them and talking with them later, it is clear that for both couple and congregation this expresses something deeply, more deeply than words. In this apparently simple action the commitment, the covenant they have made becomes somehow visible, points to this 'holy mystery in which man and woman become one flesh'.

What can we say about the service, which they have just celebrated? They have heard and assented to an understanding of marriage. An understanding of marriage as a lifelong commitment, characterized by faithfulness, mutual understanding and love. They have openly, and without coercion, made promises to each other; they have taken each other:

for better, for worse,
for richer, for poorer,
in sickness and in health,
to love and to cherish,
till death us do part.

They have received God's blessing on their marriage and they are now on their way to register legally the existence of this new reality of which the candle speaks so visibly.

What they have said and done matters: worship teaches us how to live. It is not what worship is for, but it is properly one of its consequences. So this act of worship in which Andrew and Dawn have just shared tells us something about what the Christian community thinks marriage is and how it is to be lived.

And what it tells us is something that might surprise Andrew and Dawn: that marriage is public; that marriage is for ever; that marriage is not their personal possession, nor a domestic arrangement between families; that marriage is representative – it says things to and displays things for other people; that the things it says and displays are about God, his love, and his will for creation. At the heart of it of course is Andrew and Dawn's loving relationship. The wedding marks an important step on a very personal journey. But the rite, the service places the personal in a larger world; they are invited to walk into a bigger room.

Andrew and Dawn may assent to all this with their hearts and minds (that may have been the point of the wedding preparation sessions!). But they may still be surprised by it. Surprised because this understanding of marriage – though spelt out in the words and actions of the celebration – is not an understanding of marriage that our culture could naturally endorse.

For us marriage is private, of purely personal significance. It is public in so far as it has to be registered. But a beach in the Canary Islands, a grand country house, or a drive-through chapel in Las Vegas is as appropriate a place as a church for such a celebration. Marriage is of life intention, certainly. Not only Dawn and Andrew, but also all of us mean those vows when we make them. But again meaning is a very personal business too in this culture. It bears more on what I feel and think than on anything external, anything we might call objective (an ironically slippery word for us!). If Andrew and Dawn's marriage is to be one of four out of ten that will end in divorce, that is personally sad, even tragic. But that too is regarded as a personal rather than more broadly social issue.

Andrew and Dawn see the personal nature of their relationship very clearly. Their marriage is an affirmation of their love, and an opportunity for celebration. But it is also more. They are representing and witnessing to their family, their friends and the people they work with. The marriage they are making, the vows they have exchanged, the actions that display this, the life to which it calls them: these take on a representative, sacramental function. Indeed it is precisely to articulate this that they celebrate a wedding service at all.

The Church created wedding services very intentionally. The Eucharist and the daily prayer of the Church, funeral rites and so on – these suggest themselves immediately from the pages of the New Testament alone. But wedding rites do not. We have no ancient Christian wedding rites. Certainly from early on it became customary for a married couple to come to the Eucharist and receive the bishop's blessing. But marriage was a civil affair. Above all in the ancient world it was a domestic affair which took place in and between family homes. It is a setting which showed a marked reluctance to be dragged into the ecclesiastical sphere, and priests were often seen as an unwelcome presence at the wedding celebration itself.

So when the Church creates and celebrates a wedding liturgy it is setting forth for the world a particular vision for marriage. It is a vision of marriage as a covenant, rather than simply a contract. A covenant which calls people to a mutual faithfulness. And this faithfulness has the role of a sign: as the prayers of the marriage service make clear, the marriage sums up and displays for others not just what it means to be married and the responsibilities involved. It sums up and displays (and continues to do so through the years that it is lived) something about the nature and faithfulness of God, who loves us and goes on loving us – 'for better, for worse; for richer, for poorer; in sickness and in health …'

Marriage is a mystery, a journey with and through a mystery. The journey of two people in love and friendship, in which God is encountered and experienced (even when – as for Andrew and Dawn – he is not named and recognized). More, the covenant of marriage and the way it is lived is a sign of God's love for others. The living out of that covenant that it may be such a sign makes demands of sacrificial love, self-criticism and humility on those who make their marriage vows to one another. Marriage is not a moment, but a dynamic growing and loving and serving, a way of discipleship. Marriage is not a private or even personal affair, but a public and permanent consecration, a sacrament at whose heart is the displaying and sharing of God's reconciling love for his whole creation.

So that is something about the nature of marriage. Before proceeding to discuss marriage, priesthood and ministry, I want first to develop an understanding of priesthood as a distinctive ministry among the people of God.

Priesthood as a way of being a person

When Peter was ordained priest, all he knew was that God had called him. He is now in his early sixties, and all he really knows is that God did call him and continues to call him.

He had become a Christian when he was 17, and then become involved in the life of his local Methodist church. As a student he became an Anglican, and grew to love measured and dignified worship. During his time as a student he began to put a name to something he had been feeling for years. The feeling had been very incoherent, and had been around long before he became a Christian. As he prayed and talked about it, the name he gave it was 'calling'. He was being called in some way, to fulfil some particular purpose. As a student Peter was not used to thinking like this, but began to recognize this for what it was. And gradually he began to put the word 'priest' alongside the word 'calling'. He became enormously aware that this was to be his life.

His ministry has been very varied. After ordination Peter was a curate in a mining town and then in a large 'village'; contrasting experiences that made him recognize how much context settles what we do. The work with very poor people in his first curacy contrasted very much with the genteel visits he spent most of his time doing in the second. But he was happy to be doing both. He has been a parish priest all his life – three incumbencies, all in the same diocese. The big time was 15 years in a large suburban parish, rescuing it from years of neglect and decline. Deeply rewarding years of hard work, busy days, endless demands on his time and energy. Now he is priest-in-charge of a medium-sized commuter village near the city.

Towards the end of a long ministry, Peter is reflecting on what he has done and been. He is profoundly aware of the many changes in society and Church, and of the ways these have affected the practice of his priest-hood. He is aware particularly of what many describe as the seculariza-tion of society, and the marginalization of the Christian community. He knows some of his colleagues ask questions about why they do what they do, now that so many traditional roles filled by priests have come to be done by others. Peter has been an enthusiastic encourager of lay involve-ment in the liturgical and pastoral life of the Church, and has himself rejoiced in glimpsing how such involvement has enabled people to live their faith better.

He is also deeply aware of a desire in himself not to be seen as a person apart. The twin traditions of the nineteenth century – the evangelical and catholic revivals – which have so much shaped the church in which Peter trained, both led to a redefinition of the priest as somebody separate, either as authoritative interpreter of the word of God, or as man of the sanctuary. Peter recognizes that his ministry is and should be distinctive, but feels strongly that new thinking has to be done about the relationship between the clergy and the laity, theologically, liturgically and pastorally.

Peter loves the busyness and bustle of parish life. He does not enjoy spending long hours at the word processor, but he knows that part of his ministry is to be an administrator. He has kept reading and praying and visiting. He has been diligent in keeping in touch with both the roots of his calling and the needs of his parishioners.

Throughout his ministry, Peter has sought to be a faithful priest. He has a deep sense that as a priest he is a marked man, physically, spiritually and theologically. He reads the Ordinal on the anniversary of his ordina-tion each year. The values and teaching that it enshrines have shaped his life. He takes very seriously the sense it gives that he is a representative person with a distinctive ministry, its sense of public and permanent consecration of a life.

But down the many years of his ministry, through demands made and responded to, through the pressures and stresses, Peter knows something very clearly: that the most important thing has not been anything he has done, but what he has received and what he is. His convictions and experience tell him that priesthood describes a way of being a person, rather than the doing of a series of ministerial acts. What Peter is, what he represents for others, and how this way of being is nurtured are the centre of his calling.

Peter's reflections on his ministry, and that of his friends and colleagues, have led him to a clear understanding, an understanding of a priest not so much as a person who does certain things and has certain skills but simply as a certain kind of person. It is priesthood as a way rather of being than of doing.

Peter sees that priesthood is a way of being a Christian, a way of being an adult disciple, marked, formed and nurtured in particular ways. It is marked by an intense life of prayer, by a significant proportion of each day being given to the practice of praying, of waiting on God, of talking with God, of staying on through the darkness and through the dryness. It is marked by particular ways of service within and alongside the community of which the priest is pastor, and marked by a particular role in the liturgical celebrations of that community.

And if priesthood is a particular way of being a person rather than doing certain things, it must be marked by a particular lifestyle, a life of sacrifice, a life both of voluntary and involuntary renunciation. Peter certainly finds himself amused and challenged by John Wesley's refusal to ordain anyone to the Methodist ministry who did not fast two days a week.

But the sacrifice is deeper than how much we give away or give up. Peter is deeply aware that the greatest sacrifice in his own life and ministry has been that of time, of being available, of simply being there. In many ways, time and presence are the greatest, even the only, gifts that he has had to give to others. That availability is both availability to God in worship and prayer, and availability to others in ministry. Peter – at a time when many question the way they are paid – particularly values the word 'stipend' to describe how he is paid: he is paid not to do but to be.

All of this begins to issue in a radical vision of priestly being as a sign to the world. In a world that defines human fulfilment in terms of material success, and which identifies external things as the only real things, Christians in general and priests in particular are called to make difficult choices.

A priest lives a life and exercises a ministry that cannot easily be evaluated in the world's terms, whose goals and objectives cannot really be defined. Priests have to be very clear about the problems they have to face here, in particular the temptation to be busy simply in an attempt to justify their existence. 'Success', in so far as it is any part of the priest's vocabulary, is a paradoxical thing in Christian life, for it involves losing your life in order to save it, becoming meek, being a servant, and so on. The world's notion of a successful church may be of one that is full three times a Sunday and has a great social calendar. It is frightening that some local churches are also influenced by this kind of model. The New Testament model is rather different: a successful church is one where the hungry are fed, where the naked are clothed, where the blind see, where the poor hear the Good News.

The Lord we follow, the Lord whose life we claim to share, is one whose only way to heal us was to be wounded and whose only way to real life was suffering and death. That is why – perhaps most importantly and most intangibly – the way of priesthood is a way marked with the wounds of Christ. Only one who knows in his own life the paradoxical victory of the cross, of the risen Lord who still bears the wounds of the cross, will be able to preach the gospel to others in any way.

Peter, indeed, has become deeply aware over his priestly life that others are not prepared to open their own wounds to him unless they recognize that he is a wounded person too. And people do not feel able to share their own struggles, joys and darkness in prayer and in the whole Christian life until they can recognize that he is a serious pilgrim on the way, someone who – however inadequately – is trying to follow Christ himself.

This is hard stuff, and easier to say than to live. Clergy live with all sorts of unresolved tensions – feeling overqualified and underqualified for what they do; having feelings of uselessness and unproductivity; having worries about whether what they are doing means anything. Much clerical burnout is the result of people failing to examine these tensions, and lack of appropriate support to help people do this.

Many priests need to be invited and encouraged to rediscover the roots of their calling – in their relationship with God and in their service of God's people.

Married priesthood

Andrew and Dawn on the one hand and Peter on the other point to something about marriage and something about priesthood. They both share in the notion of 'holy mystery', expressed through the sacraments. Both marriage and priesthood are states of life entered into with life intention. They are both ways that are best talked about not in terms of doing but of being. And they both have a representative, symbolic nature and function, a quality of witness to another set of values than those current in society.

Some case studies

I am going to talk about four clergy marriages. Each illustrates a very different way of seeking to live with the mystery of marriage and priesthood. These case studies are based on real clergy couples, though it is worth remembering that in any such study there is a degree of caricature.

Robert and Val illustrate the traditional clergy marriage successfully reinterpreted on their own terms. Josie and Stan are a couple seeking to cross traditional barriers, and hitting some problems. Reg and Margaret show how the traditional blueprint can go disastrously wrong. Philip and Lucy show that if you get your calling right, God will do the rest.

Robert and Val

Robert and Val are in their late forties now. Robert has been a priest for 21 years. For the first 15 he was single. His singleness had never been a positive life choice, but he was comfortable with it. When he met Val, there were a variety of issues to face. Val had already been married and was now divorced. Her two children were at college, but emotionally very tied to her.

As they became closer, Robert and Val had to think hard about the nature of their relationship. They had to sort out whether getting married was the right thing. Val had come to Christian faith as an adult, but long before she met Robert. They both took traditional Christian teaching about marriage and divorce very seriously. They were also very clear that their marriage would have to be understood within the context of Robert's priestly life and ministry.

After some difficulty, Robert and Val married. Six years on it is a very happy and stable relationship. Val works part-time as a pharmacist. She has also taken on many 'traditional' roles as the vicar's wife. However, she is very clear that this is something she has chosen and feels is part of her calling as a human being.

Val enjoys living in a vicarage. She finds the interruptions and the life of people around her exciting and encouraging. She has taken part in parish study groups and so forth, and feels accepted as herself, a person in her own right. Hers is not a role assumed, but an identity she feels and knows is hers. Their Christian community and the wider parish clearly glimpse in Robert and Val something very rooted and committed. Their life together speaks to others of possibilities. Val's previous marriage is something she can openly talk about. As far as she is concerned she has developed a sense of who she is that makes her strong enough to be clear about why she is fulfilling the traditional role. It is not important what she does in her Christian community; what is important is that she retains her sense of self and can relate to the other Christians on her terms.

The crucial factor is that they are doing what is right for them. When a married couple is faced with the enormous burden of historical association, it is vital that the personal calling is as strong as iron. Only then can you face the possibilities and pitfalls of living in a vicarage.

Josie and Stan

Josie has felt from childhood that she is called to be a priest. She comes from a traditional Christian family. Although her background has given her the words to voice her calling, it has also provided the greatest obstacles to its fulfilment. Her family at first found it very difficult to support her calling to the priesthood, though to her joy this has now changed. Probably the most moving moment of her life was when her father – himself a priest – received communion at her first mass.

Josie and Stan met at university and married very soon after graduation. At that point Josie felt unable to offer herself for training for ordination even though she clearly felt called to the priesthood. That was not then a possibility. She did a PGCE and started teaching while Stan finished his medical studies. They were both committed members of their local church, but Josie felt diffident about being over-involved. The reason she gave for this was the busyness of teaching. Inside she was aware of a degree of anger that inhibited her from feeling fully part of the life of the Christian community.

After three years the sense of dislocation had become intolerable. Stan had begun work as a GP, something he had always wanted to do and loved. Josie was both unhappy as a teacher and envious of the evident delight Stan took in his work. She made enquiries about ordained ministry – as a deaconess, the only thing on offer. She was astounded to discover that the local area bishop did not approve of married deaconesses. That felt like one further kick in the face.

However, with Stan's help and the enthusiastic (though sometimes highly insensitive) support of her parish priest, Josie persevered and was accepted for training. She trained at a residential college 35 miles from home – staying at college through most of the week and going home at weekends. It was unsatisfactory and stressful but probably the only practical solution. Stan was really supportive, but she felt the strain.

Josie was ordained in 1987, just when it became possible for women to be deacons. That did not make it much easier when a year later all the men with whom she had been made deacon were ordained priest. She served a five-year curacy in a large town in a parish with a team of three clergy. Stan's GP practice was 15 miles away and the logistics worked well.

Josie became deacon-in-charge of a modern church in a middle-class housing development. Within 18 months she had been ordained priest and installed as incumbent. Four years on she feels there is some stability. The network of women clergy in the diocese has been of enormous importance to her. She has been delighted to receive the friendship and support of the local Roman Catholic priest. She still feels ill at ease at some clergy chapter meetings. She loves going to Benediction, but has not felt over-welcome when she has gone to Benediction in the nearby parish.

Josie is very strong and has lived most of her life with a clear vision of what God is calling her to do. Despite this, and the large amount of support she has received, she still feels there are questions over her legitimacy. This raises its head particularly in the context of her marriage. Stan has always been very supportive. But then Josie thinks he might have been very supportive if she had wanted to be a Buddhist. She feels he has not understood just how much following her call has cost her, and continues to cost. His support has been crucial, and yet she remains in some doubt as to how seriously Stan takes what she does and is.

Stan for his part does feel curiously ambivalent. He rather enjoys his novel status in the congregation as the vicar's husband. He is struck by the fact that people expect him to be quite a passive person and are sometimes surprised to discover that he has a job. But Josie is right, although they never talk about it: he is interested in the fact that his wife is a priest, but feels somewhat detached from it. He is aware that Josie is deeply fulfilled now in a way she was not as a teacher, but does not reflect on this very much. When he answers the phone to a parishioner or the local undertaker, he is fascinated by the particularity of the conversations he has, but finds it difficult to see that this is part of the mainstream of life. He admires his wife's work, but often feels she is in training for something else.

Josie and Stan have a good marriage in a general way. It is well rooted and they have supported each other through a great deal. They both live with a sense that they have crossed boundaries and done something rather different from their contemporaries. But if their marriage and Josie's ministry are going to continue vibrant and exciting, there needs to be a greater reckoning between them of who they are before God and who they are called to be together for others. Otherwise the current lack of serious understanding between them may easily develop into very separate professional careers.

Reg and Margaret

Reg and Margaret have been married for ten years; they met at college and married some years later. Until four years ago Reg worked for a large homelessness charity. Both Reg and Margaret were heavily involved at their local church. Originally Reg had come to faith in an independent

Pentecostal church, but had become an Anglican when he married Margaret.

In their Christian community there had been a great deal of emphasis on every-member ministry. In practice this had led to a whole series of active men from the congregation seeking ordination. Reg was one of them.

Margaret was happy to support Reg in this. They were a praying household. They did not have any children, and Margaret had played a very active role in the life of the church for some years – youth group, nurture group, prayer group. In many ways her involvement in the liturgical and ministerial life of the church had been greater than Reg's. As far as she could see, the sphere of Reg's Christian ministry was very much his work with homeless people. She was surprised, but quite happy when he began to talk about ordination.

After two very swift years at theological college, Reg was ordained deacon and they moved to a prosperous suburban parish for his curacy. Very soon Margaret felt much was wrong. She had some part-time work, and Reg was very disciplined about a day off each week. But their ministry and spiritual life together evaporated. They no longer prayed together, and Margaret felt not so much subordinate as irrelevant. The house felt very lonely. The folk at church, although welcoming, clearly found it confusing that she should actually want to be involved in any deeper way than simply being there on a Sunday morning. She found what she saw of Reg's new role – liturgical and pastoral – very difficult to reconcile with what she knew of him and their relationship.

Reg actually knows this, and feels it himself. But it is impossible for him to talk with Margaret about this. It is partly his background, partly the sacrifices that Margaret has made, partly just his surprise that he feels like this. He senses – especially when he is trying to pray – that there should have been more questions asked. He is unclear about what is going on in his marriage and unclear about whether he should be ordained to the priesthood.

Reg is also feeling confusion about blurred boundaries; he is still trying to support some of his old clients from his work with homeless people. In fact, these people have become increasingly important to him. On one level he feels good that he is still important to them. But in a deeper way they give him a sense of self-worth that he does not experience in his marriage or in his active ministry. In his marriage he feels barren. In his active ministry he feels both deeply incompetent and very distant. This contrasts very much with his experience as an active lay Christian.

Some of this may be passing phases of adjustment. But there is a serious disjunction between Reg and Margaret's calling as a married couple and the priestly ministry to which Reg feels called and to which Margaret has given her assent. All along the way, everyone involved has given insufficient attention to the difference between priestly ministry and an active lay vocation.

Because one calling has gone awry it has threatened and undermined the other existing calling of marriage. There is a problem with the priestly ministry – not that it is over-honoured but that lay ministry is undervalued. Reg realized he had a calling, and that because it was a calling it had to be in ordained priestly ministry. Tragically his zeal to serve the Lord has led two devout Christians into a confusing mass of pain and resentment.

There are certainly many personal issues here for Reg and Margaret to face up to. Out of that may come a renewed vision of their Christian life and ministry. Also it is important to recognize that the journey of and to priesthood is one marked for many by pain and problems. However, Reg and Margaret's story also raises serious structural issues about how the church selects and trains candidates, and what appropriate support and challenge is offered in that process.

Philip and Lucy

Philip and Lucy live on a large council estate. Their vicarage is the only detached house on the estate. That is not quite accurate because it is in fact attached to the church and parish hall within a single enclosure. They have four small children, all less than six years old.

Philip has felt called to the priesthood from childhood. It has been a constant fact of his life for as long as he can remember. He grew up in a traditional congregation, and has been actively involved in liturgical ministry from the age of five. He has developed a rich and sincere devotional life that centres on the daily office, daily Eucharist and an hour's silence each day. During his time at university and theological college he considered seriously whether he was called to a celibate vocation.

Lucy and Philip met at a social in the club in the parish where Lucy worked as a probation officer. Lucy was not and is not a practising Christian. She is deeply involved in many women's groups and had been a probation officer for four years when she met Philip.

To Philip it was an unusual romance and courtship. It took them both very much by surprise, because they seemed to come from such different worlds. Some of the congregation where Philip was curate found it very difficult to relate to Lucy through the two years following their marriage. Philip was their young and devout curate. He did not stop being young or devout. But their understanding of who he was changed absolutely.

Philip then became team vicar in a large inner-city parish, and they had a whole series of children. The fact that Lucy does not share Philip's faith was seen as problematic by some. But their visible, sincere commitment to one another, and Lucy's passionate concern about the renewal of the estate somehow puts things in a different context.

In their personal life, faith is something central between them. Philip recognizes in Lucy a person of real faith – but a faith expressed in social action and which does not readily refer to God or the Christian tradition. Lucy likewise knows Philip's faith to be sincere and real, and something that is not a sealed-off area but one that affects everything that he does and is. They have developed a custom of giving each other times of silence. In the loft of their vicarage they have created a silent space. For half an hour each day, while one minds the children and the telephone, the other makes use of the loft.

Philip has developed a strong daily mass in the church, and knows it to be the springboard of his ministry. He delights in the insights Lucy gives him about the community, about society, about himself and their relationship. He knows that some of his colleagues find his marriage baffling because Lucy is very clearly not a Christian. But he is deeply happy in his marriage and as a priest, and he and Lucy feel a complete congruity between these callings.

In contrast to the confusion and potential disaster that threatens Reg and Margaret, Lucy and Philip show how clarity of purpose and of calling can give the space in which a marriage can thrive. They have both been true to their separate callings and remarkably today we can see how God is continually present, weaving his presence through their separate and mutual lives.

Conclusion to the case studies

In these case studies we have seen a variety of patterns, a variety of ways of living out the mystery of priesthood and the mystery of marriage. There is inevitably no single model or blueprint, and there is a degree of contradiction both within and between the examples we have looked at. But some core themes do emerge: the importance of spiritual discipline; the necessity in priesthood and marriage of living with visions of what we may be and with realism about what we are; and the glorious truth that all is redeemable.

Marriage, priesthood and prophecy

In all of this, we need to be broad in our vision – of marriage and priesthood, and of married priesthood. The world in which these realities exist is in rapid change. Wisdom and vision need to be applied for the well-being and appropriate development of these sacraments if they are truly to be what they are intended to be in the economy of God.

Many discussions of clergy marriage have been negative and critical in tone. Their focus is the practical reality of vicarage life, etc. These are important areas. There are tensions around such issues as housing, pay, children, time off, the boundaries between public and private, and working space. These tensions are right, appropriate and part of any good marriage. And in clergy marriage, just as in any other ordinary marriage, these things must be thrashed out as you go along, and not lost in high-minded notions of inappropriate self-sacrifice and spiritual heroism.

Real prophecy is about being yourself in the Lord. Otherwise the symbolic, representative nature of priesthood and of marriage can be severely compromised. However – as the stories of Reg and Margaret and to a different degree Josie and Stan indicate – who you are in the calling to priesthood and who you are in the calling to marriage may be in conflict. The resolution and to some extent containment of such conflict is very hard, and the current divorce rate among clergy – especially those ordained later in life – is indicative of this. There is a need here for much disciplined thinking by those responsible for the nurturing and formation of priests and those charged with their pastoral care. It is at any rate clear that there needs to be a strengthening of support given to priests, married or not, and a more open debate with and within congregations about the pressures that are around.

If all we have said about marriage and priesthood is the case, then the hallmarks of married priesthood are prophetic witness, sacrifice and service, underpinned by a commitment to a serious life of prayer. This is not about interior piety but about all the details of life. Just as in a monastic community the leader might also be found cleaning the toilets, so in a priest's family. If he is a male priest, he shares in the broken nights when the children are small; he changes nappies as readily as his wife; he disciplines his time well so the family eat together, and so forth.

This is particularly important as part of the enacted prophecy of married male priests. It is quite clear that in households where both partners work, the wife still bears a disproportionate responsibility for the domestic duties. The simple comment of one priest's wife recently says it all: 'During the day I am a nurse; when I get home I am a housewife and mother.' The notion that sharing in the running of a household is alien to, or outside the scope of, priestly living is a tragic perversion. If this whole business of priesthood is about a way of being a person, and if the context of that way is marriage, then every part of daily life is brought within the sphere of our calling. We have not had many years to reflect on the experience of married women priests and their spouses. Anecdotal evidence so far suggests that responsibilities are negotiated with rather greater care.

We are challenged here to a vision of priestly holiness and of married holiness. It is a vision that finds echoes in the poetry of George Herbert, and deep roots in the rule of St Benedict. It is a vision that may well find its patterns very different from those assumed in the tradition. A priest may find that he says Morning Prayer with his family at 8.30 a.m. rather than alone in church two hours earlier. As we have seen, sustainable patterns are necessary, and only if they are sustainable will they be sustaining. Inappropriate patterns of praying, or those too rigidly imposed will not simply be unhelpful but will create and feed hurt and division. In thinking this through, priests have to learn to respect the spiritual lives of their spouses and to give space for their nurture. Such things as the honouring of daily silence – as we saw with Philip and Lucy – will make demands on both partners. And that is how it should be if we are seeking to live out these complementary vocations.

Maybe in our work-addicted society, there is no more important area in fashioning the married priest's household according to the way of Christ than that of time. We said earlier that in a sense all a priest has is time. And yet many clergy are so threatened by an empty diary that their lives are filled up with activities that they should not be doing. In the life of a married priest it is of enormous importance that the arteries are unclogged from this kind of thinking. A youth worker from the Mar Thoma Church in South India has said: 'Yes, it is the same in India. All the priests are too fat because they don't have enough time to exercise.' Rates of early retirement through sickness and of physical and psychological burnout among clergy are indicative enough. But the youth worker's comment spoke not simply of physical fitness but of a whole inappropriate approach to priestly ministry.

Patterns of holiday, time off, quiet, silence, and relaxation are part of the fundamental framework every bit as much as daily prayer. Without these patterns we simply mirror back to the world its own confusion.

Again, this is easy to say and hard to do. Daily, weekly and yearly patterns are hard to establish, and flexibility is essential. But the patterns must be there if we are to do more than simply survive. Father John Gaskill once remarked that the reason so many of the old Cowley Fathers were such holy people is that when it was their turn for silence someone else answered the door. This kind of thinking needs to be applied to the development of appropriate patterns of holiday, study, work and rest. Clergy ringing round their colleagues to get Sunday cover the week before they fly off on a holiday they booked six months before is reprehensible bad management (we know; we have been there!).

Conclusion

It is important to emphasize that priests and their spouses are human beings. They live as members of society and are touched and made by that society. They are not (and cannot be) immune to social trends and values and attitudes. Indeed, a priest cannot be because (as Thomas Aquinas pointed out) the 'world', along with the Scriptures and the sacraments, is one of the three sources of theological reflection. More than this, if priests are to stand at the crossroads of many different people's lives and be appropriate interpreters of their experience then it is essential that they are deeply immersed in the facts and realities that make both them-selves and others what they are.

In our society, the media (in their broadest sense) very much occupy the role of the medieval church in terms of creating our value systems and signalling what is legitimate. Part of being a priest is to engage in a creative and prophetic dialogue with the prevailing values of the wider community with wisdom and understanding.

As Christian sacraments, marriage and priesthood are means of grace for the people involved in them, and they are ways in which God touches, heals and challenges others. This is clear enough in the texts of the ordi-nation services, and in the prayers of the marriage services: 'Strengthen them with your grace that they may be witnesses of Christ to others'; 'May their life together witness to your love in this troubled world; may unity overcome division, forgiveness heal injury, and joy triumph over sorrow.'

In a society where the popular reception of existentialism and other movements have made people question the possibility (and even desir-ability) of life commitments at a basic level, then part of the priestly role of the married priest and of the married Christian is to witness (in a way every bit as radical and prophetic as celibacy) to a different set of values, a different way of looking at the world. This is where the representative nature of priesthood and the representative nature of marriage meet. They reveal their quality and value as living witness.

We may stand for high notions of what a priest is in the community, but this can be almost impossible to sustain as a public witness: we have to struggle hard as flesh-and-blood human beings, faced with conflicting pressures from society and the Church, to hold all aspects of our selves together in a life that can be lived with integrity; this is especially true in the area of sexuality.

8
The Priest, Sex and Society

PETER ALLAN CR

Priesthood and marriage are uniquely powerful images. Both speak of stability, love and dedication. Both have been raised up by romantic ideals and brought down by scandal and disgrace. Both have an irreplaceable contribution to make within the Christian community and beyond it. Yet just as our understanding of both has seen constant renewal and change, now there is a new urgency. We need new ways of speaking about the meeting between ideals and reality. How can the ideal of lifelong marriage survive the statistics for marital breakdown? How can priesthood enable those ordained to such ministry to go on being fallible humans and yet represent the infallible God? What are the limits to such tensions, and how are we to understand them in our generation?

For such reasons, writing about priesthood today must inevitably touch on those areas of human life that are generally contentious or problematic. The relation between the distinct and special character of the priesthood and the things that we all share as human beings has changed – and is still changing. A certain kind of theology, a certain kind of social construction encouraged a myth of priesthood. In such a myth, the priest became a strange fantasy creature who cannot be imagined engaging in the mundane business of life – going to the toilet, going shopping, making love. The social changes that we have witnessed in the last 50 years demand a reassessment, but it has proved hard to find ways of bringing together those things that mark priests out and those that constitute their solidarity with everyone else. Issues of sexuality and gender loom large in present discussion, and we shall focus on some of these issues, but first something needs to be said of the larger context.

Changing world, changing roles

With hindsight, the second half of the last century looks increasingly like a time of transition. In many ways, those 50 years in Britain and much of Europe represent the necessary adjustment and adaptation imposed by the two world wars. It is not that much of the social change that we have witnessed would not have happened without the experiences of war, but those two cataclysmic events determined so largely the context for the social change. From time to time, the various realignments required that different groups in society underwent a 'makeover'. The Anglican clergy, along with priests and ministers of other traditions in Britain, have been drawn into such self-appraisal, though generally reactively and cautiously. Towards the end of the century, two popular portrayals of priests and the Church brought many of the questions and issues to the fore in a way that would, just ten years before, have been inconceivable. McGovern's film *Priest*, and the subsequent television serial *The Lakes* brought into the open a conversation that was still barely whispered behind closed doors.

Times when change is very evident always produce particular tensions. The rate of change has been so fast that some, ordained at a time when the shape of things seemed near immutable, are now incapable of re-imagining their role. They continue, and offer valuable ministry, but their interpretative frame of reference is to be found in a world that has now disappeared. Others, aware of the changes around them, have become disabled. Nothing serves to undergird their self-understanding. The very possibility of continuing a priestly ministry appears to have been denied them. Others again have been eager to seize the possibilities of the moment and have been creative and charismatic, but have had problems with the necessary continuities of a faith rooted in history and tradition.

Vocation – shapes and models

Astonishingly, men and women still experience a strong sense of being called to ordained ministry in a way that, at least in the early stages, seems to them realizable. This sense of being called to something that can be envisioned may persist until after ordination, sometimes well into ordained life. Later, however, many find themselves caught in a maelstrom of conflicting expectations, temptations, lures and possibilities. There is now little sense that the shape of being a priest is to be found as some-thing held by the Church; little sense that there is some core manner of living the life of the priest to which all can and should approximate. Rather, there is a strong sense that each must mould themselves according to their gifts, convictions and situations. Yet there is also an awareness of a persistent 'should': that the Church *should* have expectations of her priests that amount to a role that all can fulfil. At the same time, when-ever the Church makes some statement that touches intimately on the lives of priests, there is an equally strong sense that the Church *cannot* speak authoritatively in this way without coming into conflict with each priest's proper pursuit of an authentic life.

It does not take much reflection to see how this has affected the way that priests and their families have participated in the search for meaning and value with their contemporaries. Less confident of the 'society' of the Church, the vicarage family is less likely to comply with the caricatures, less likely to be dressed from the parish jumble sale, more likely to shop at Harvey Nicholls and Marks & Spencer. Similarly, attitudes to working hours, to the use of the vicarage as an office and meeting place, to the 'right' to a private life – all these reflect a shift from a confidence that the Church in its relation to the wider society was capable of ordering and addressing these matters and supporting her priests in what was not infrequently described as 'a life of sacrifice'. It is important to note that it is precisely a shift *from* confidence, much more than it is a shift *to* anything very clear.

There were models of 'being a priest', handed down from generation to generation, but even where the models mean something to those entering upon ordained ministry, they are no longer obvious to many in the Church and the society around us. The times are especially confusing because there is no one way of reading them. Some plod on with extraordinary faithfulness, as though it will all come right again soon; some give up, faced with the indifference and incomprehension; some launch out on what seems often to their friends to be a path of incredible idiosyncrasy. The problem is experienced at the spiritual, liturgical, theological, moral and social levels. It is proper to speak of crisis, but in the New Testament sense: a moment of decision and judgement, a moment of God. It is not a disastrous moment, not a time of catastrophe, no matter how much of what we now know and treasure is going to disappear in the generations to come. For Christians committed irrevocably to the centrality of the incarnation, this time, this history is God's time and God's history – as the prophet Isaiah has it: 'My word ... shall not return to me empty, but it shall accomplish that which I purpose, and prosper in the thing for which I sent it' (Isa. 55.11, RSV).

Yet this is a real turning point for all that, and one that is not going to go away – despite the fact that priests perhaps more than anyone else in the Church tend to take the ostrich line. The Federation of the Evangelical Churches in the former German Democratic Republic, responding to the WCC report *Baptism, Eucharist and Ministry*, said in 1988, 'The crisis in which the ordained ministry finds itself today in the world and in the church ... is an indispensable part of every discussion on the ministry.' They went on to say that ordained ministers themselves sense a 'lack of assurance, or a loss of certainty as to the significance and shape of their ministry'. The difficulties are compounded, they believe, because of 'a widely observable refusal to acknowledge the reality of this situation' and an 'administrative rigidity' preventing effective response.[1] Much in the rich tradition that has formed so many priests says, 'In times of adversity and turmoil, stick to the disciplines and patterns you have learnt and wait ...' But the urgent need is for change, for new life is coming at us from all directions and the Spirit must not be resisted. John Collins, in his small follow-up to *Diakonia*, entitled *Are all Christians Ministers?* gives some startling statistics in the early pages.[2] In 1991, official Roman Catholic statistics reported that 73 per cent of all priests reside in Europe and North America, caring for just 38 per cent of the world's Roman Catholics. And of 174 priests in the Seattle diocese, only half were expected to be still serving in the year 2000.

We have become familiar with a model of priesthood, with a pattern of relationships within the body of Christ. It is a pattern that has brought many blessings to priests and people alike. It has its icons of holiness, its heroes and anti-heroes, but it is changing; indeed, not just changing, but passing away.

Paradoxically, outside the Church there is sometimes a clearer shape to the expectations laid upon the ordained, both genuine and distorted: the media continue to articulate the task of the priest in a way that many would recognize. That they do so in a way suggestive of a caste of miracle workers who are doomed to fail does not alter the fact that they touch on something of the inner mystery of the life of the priest. The priest is to speak when others cannot. The priest is to interpret, to care, to heal, and to connect the often-tragic events of daily life to the transcendent possibilities. The priest is to make sense of the fragments of the lives of others, though the priest's own life is not more evidently united or meaningful. The ambiguity implicit here is well discussed by Kenneth Mason in his *Priesthood and Society*.[3] The particular privileges of entering into a tradition such as Christian priesthood, with its vast line of history and experience, is now more usually encountered as burden rather than possibility.

Seeking integrity

Those who are seeking to live as bishops, priests and deacons in this generation are also powerfully influenced by the values, goals and ambitions of their friends and neighbours. To a large extent there is neither time, nor opportunity, nor, sometimes, inclination to see where this results in a conflict with the claims of the gospel – and particularly as those have been received and lived by the Church of England. Commonly, life is lived under pressure and, as in natural selection, the strongest forces win. There is, in such a context, a particularly acute risk of the loss of integrity, of living parallel lives.

Above all, it illustrates the culture of untruth and deception in which so much of our lives is set. These distorted ways of carrying on have come to achieve validity, a certain sad correctness. That this should be so has been thoroughly explored by a weighty strain of philosophical reflection beginning in the early 1980s with Alasdair MacIntyre's *After Virtue*.[4] MacIntyre's analysis and his exploration of contemporary fragmentation and the tendency to 'emotivism' furnishes some understanding of the way in which it has become possible for us to operate in little, discrete boxes – pretending the left hand does not know what the right hand is doing; and also the way in which, in such a situation (for other more complex reasons too) we have become detached from coherent traditions of moral life and resort more and more to doing what I believe to be right for me without reference to others. MacIntyre's picture is a gloomy one. Indeed, he famously concludes at one point that 'it is no longer possible, strictly speaking, to be moral'! In the 1990s more hopeful responses began to emerge and some of the work of the Roman Catholic philosopher Charles Taylor[5] has taken up the notion of authenticity (and the linked notion of integrity) which has a strong resonance for us in the present discussion. We should certainly wish for priests of integrity; those who are priests wish to be so with integrity, to live an authentic priestly life. There is no reason to doubt the sincerity of these desires, but how are they to be realized? What is needed first is an acknowledgement of the way in which adherence to these goals is coloured and compromised by being inalienably of our generation. And in this generation authenticity too often means no more than, 'It feels right to me.' And when we say, 'It belongs to my integrity to …' we mean, 'I am going to impose what I take to be my right …'

And from the perspective of the priest we have to acknowledge a particular ambiguity. There was a time when it at least seemed possible to admit of no separation between being a priest of Christ's Church and a person of one's times. Not so today. The demand now is for priesthood to be specially characterized by an acknowledgement of participation in the search for the goals of authenticity and integrity, but in such a way as to set before ourselves, the Church and our neighbours a dynamic new realization of the gospel call to forsake all and follow Christ. It is not that we are afraid of the call to sacrifice – rather that, as usual, we are not so keen to make it in the way that Christ asks of us. In an age when the distortions of self-centred individualism are beginning to be recognized, there is a special onus on the priests of the Church to demonstrate by their life and actions that while their ministry, as an extension of their baptism, is given and empowered by Christ, it is also given to them by and on behalf of the whole Church to whom they are accountable. Second, they have to ensure that their personal lives – because of the particular character of Christian priesthood – are free of the kind of schizophrenia that we sometimes see where there is no true integrity and connection between the priest on duty and the person at leisure. Third, it is important that they are willing and content to be models of Christian life for others – and implicit in this is a willingness to seek to embody patterns of Christian living that can be realistically adopted by men and women much more bound by the conditions of the secular world.

Portraying the priest

Against this backdrop, McGovern's film *Priest* emerges as a powerful testimony to one way of reading the situation. In the perhaps necessarily distorted view of the camera, we are faced with a series of unmistakably 'real' cameos: the pastorally able, socially committed priest whose house-keeper is his lover; the key parish family in which the father, a communicant member of the Church, is sexually abusing his daughter; and the curate who struggles to contain his homosexuality within his commitment to celibacy, although it is clear that he has never faced himself at sufficient depth until he allows himself to be drawn into a relationship that he lacks the freedom to sustain.

Part of the tragedy of the film is that the young man with whom the curate becomes involved is, in so many ways, a priest to the curate: with astonishing generosity in the circumstances he seeks to create a space in which the confused and foolish curate can find meaning. This generosity itself then becomes one of the elements in the conflict: it becomes impossible to discern where the greater good lies, and part of the final irony is that no one emerges with greater moral integrity than this same, flawed, young man.

It would be a mistake to read this film simply as a piece of propaganda or as a contribution to the debate. Where it succeeds most powerfully is in conveying the violent character of the dilemma in which so many find themselves. Many, if not most, want to live in a way that corresponds to their deepest knowledge and self-understanding. At the same time, they long for that to be endorsed by those they hold dear – by family and friends, by the Church, by colleagues at work, by society at large. It is at this point that some of the tensions become unbearable. In a quite new way, we have become turned back upon ourselves. Unless we are the guarantors of our own authenticity we are liable to feel coerced and constrained. But unless we are able to receive authenticity from others we are liable to feel insecure and unsatisfied.

The priest today stands alongside everyone else in this. There is no privileged space, no lofty peak on which to stand, able to minister to others while resting secure 'in tune with heaven'. The sense of the priest being somehow 'above it all' may survive to some degree where priestly celibacy is required, but is simply impossible in those churches whose ordained ministers perforce share fully with their neighbours in the business of daily living.

The gift of sex

For reasons both obvious and obscure, much of the present questioning is focused on sexuality. The sexual morality of the priest is then of particular importance because the priest is, in a particular way, the bearer of the Christian tradition, and also (even if in a diluted sense) an exemplar of human living. Contemporary media exposure of the private lives of individuals has done little to help, for it has strengthened the myth that it is possible to know all there is to know. Yet human sexuality operates on at least three levels. There is the innermost layer, the realm of magination and fantasy, the secret interpretations of the heart – a level at which we remain capable of shocking and surprising ourselves. There is the layer of private expression – a level which normally applies to the intimacy shared between two people and which is contained in their acting and speaking together, although this has its public dimension in the overflowing of love. Then there is the public level, which is normally confined to talk about sex and its expression. If ever one were to doubt the reality of sin, the human capacity to hold these three levels apart and distinct would quickly dispel it!

In its mixture of brilliance and idiosyncrasy, Michel Foucault's *History of Sexuality* both invented a way of speaking about the task of being human and also articulated what was becoming clearer to more and more people.[6] We do recognize that the very notion of sexuality has been developed as a strategy for having and using power over others. In the light of Foucault's discussion and other commentaries we begin to see the constraining, limiting force of the terminology of sexual distinction. We do recognize that there is here something very modern. Yet, at this point in our history, we seem inevitably bound to describe ourselves not simply as sexual beings but as homosexual or heterosexual, bisexual, non-sexual – or some other variation on the theme. Further, our corporate confidence in what constitutes the goods of human life is so varied, so confused, that we have tried to find clarity in the ways in which we articulate the relation between human authenticity and sexual life. The evidence for this is all too familiar, most obviously in the public hysteria over the presence of convicted sexual offenders in local communities. This has been particularly disastrous for the Christian churches: the Church has been effectively disabled from speaking at all. Pronouncements by Christian leaders appear all too often as speech from another planet. This would not necessarily be serious or bad, except that those speaking are participants in the same experience, and charges of hypocrisy are too easily laid because the pronouncements do not take on the shape of the questions as contemporary life presses them upon us.

At this stage in the discussion we must note that the Church is caught on the horns of another dilemma. What kind of response does the present require? Is this a moment for the Christian Church to hold fast? To restate traditional Christian sexual morality and seek to resist the changes that many are urging? Or is this the moment to demonstrate Christianity's capacity for reformation, a time for the liberals to triumph? Once the debate is cast in these terms, key elements of the question are lost. The restatement of the traditional view has now ceased to be able to hold within its embrace a significant number of Christians who are serious, devout and thoughtful – and, what is more, are often holding positions for the sake of others rather than themselves. On the other side, there is no sign of a meaningful consensus to support radical change. Theologically this is serious, for it lays the Church open to the charge of being incapable of contributing constructively but, instead, of reacting either positively to endorse changes that have come to dominate in a society or negatively in opposing such changes. There is no sharper example than the issue of ordaining homosexual persons and acknowledging their freedom to express their sexuality in meaningful relationships. At the same time there is need for a truthful recognition of the extent of sinful distortion in the lives, hearts and minds of those who apparently conform to the standards that traditional Christian morality approves.

Given such diversity of opinion, conviction and experience, what might we hope for? There is no lack of passion, no lack of courage in proclaiming opposing positions. But are we not aware how unsatisfactory it all is? The mixture of shock, disappointment and relief that greeted the 1998 Lambeth Conference statements is sufficient indicator. No one can be said to have 'won', and little, if anything, has been gained. I want to suggest three kinds of engagement that seem fundamental to proper Christian discourse and which have direct implications for our concerns with questions of sexuality and the priesthood.

Discretio

Why begin with a word that is not even English? *Discretio* is one of the key words in the monastic Rule of St Benedict. Pondered and lived by generations of monks and nuns, it has come to acquire rich layers of meaning. It is hugely important for describing something essential about the whole business of life together in the body of Christ. It is not at all about discretion as we usually mean it. It is that virtue, rooted in the sense of wonder that Christ is present in the world, and particularly in our companions along the way, that encourages us to be open, reverent, attentive and receptive. This presence of Christ is not a selective presence – 'All guests are to be welcomed as Christ'[7] – nor does it permit us to acknowledge Christ in only those aspects or characteristics of others that we find acceptable. First comes the reverence in the face of the other and the silence that permits an exchange of truth. Only when a true apprehension of the other has taken root in us can fruitful debate take place. Such an attitude is quite different from the popular tag 'love the sinner, hate the sin', for it involves us in an adventure of discovery that may lead to the revelation that our definitions are inadequate. This is a necessary and fundamental starting point. From the contemporary point of view, it has the advantage of beginning with interpersonal encounter, but it is not to be confused with a helplessly relativist stance. It is about the openness that the gospel requires me to show in the face of the other, but it is about my relationship with each person as that relationship is described by my life in Christ. It is the life of Christ that is the measure; it is the life of Christ that *discretio* permits us to discern in the life of the other. It is important that this is rightly understood: this exercise of *discretio* is not a thinly veiled tactic for the acceptance of a variety of sexual practices. It is rather about the proper and necessary self-emptying before the mystery of another person that is prior to the application of any standards of morality, no matter how compelling they may be in themselves.

Living tradition

The second necessary engagement is with the traditions, practices and documents of the Church. Here, the emphasis is on 'Church'. It is with the traditions, practices and documents of a fellowship, a community, that we are concerned. And, still more importantly, it is as community, as a fellowship of those united with Christ in baptism that we are to read and learn from such traditions, practices and documents. Clearly, there are many implications here. First, all who are baptized into Christ, though yet sinners, are to be treated with equal seriousness. Not all have equal authority, although it must not be forgotten that the exercise of authority in the community of Christ is a ministry of service which depends on those with oversight knowing the wisdom that belongs to *discretio* and seeking to live in the mutual obedience of which Ephesians speaks: 'Be subject to one another out of reverence for Christ' (Eph. 5.21, RSV). One of the practical consequences of such an exercise is a renewed appreciation of the virtue of patience. At such a time as this, when differing opinions and convictions are so evident, it requires a graced patience to ensure that the community of Christ is not constrained by anything less than the freedom of the Spirit. In the aftermath of the 1998 Lambeth Conference this demands urgent attention, not least because it is evident that the Christians in the northern and the southern hemispheres are not at the same point in their journeying with Christ. They cannot, as a consequence, do justice to the truth of Christ by seeking to squeeze their differing gifts into the small funnel of a common statement.

A holy ideal

The third engagement, I would suggest, must be with all that is and has been understood by the ideal of Christian marriage. In this information age, a superabundance of evidence powerfully persuades us that ideals are sheer folly. Against the odds, we are called to reaffirm the grace that can and does belong uniquely to Christian marriage as a sign of God's love and fidelity towards his people. Those who marry 'in the sight of God' choose to embody this ideal on behalf of the world. Failure should not, and does not, surprise us, but nor must it diminish the force of the ideal. If such a reading is true, I suggest that this frees the Church to be more honest in public about the wealth of human relationships – sexual, celibate and in friendship – that are being lived out by those who seek only to be faithful disciples of Christ. Because they do not, and should not, seek to partake of the sacramental ideal that belongs to Christian marriage means that they cannot be judged by the same standards. Certainly, they must be judged by Christ and the claims of the gospel, but it is terribly apparent that the Church is failing many at the present time – many whose manner of relating one to another and whose use of sexuality is in need of repentance and reform, and many whose ways of relating and whose sexual practice cries out rather for understanding and affirmation, even if this includes a recognition that the gospel demands still more of them.

Christians, surely, have an unenviable task in that they are called to 'be perfect, as your heavenly Father is perfect' and not to be 'slightly improved' as Iris Murdoch was once tempted to rephrase the demand. This, coupled with the fact that 'all have sinned and have fallen short of the glory of God', means that there will be a persistent mismatch between what we hope for one another, what we ask of ourselves, and what we actually do. In our generation such untidiness is apparently less acceptable than before. As Alasdair MacIntyre put it, we have sacrificed overall cohesion for internal coherence, and this has led to an obsession with a narrow, clearly defined accord between word and deed that cannot adequately embrace our reality. The catch-22 in this is that bearing with weakness becomes toleration of abuse; a firm stand for morality becomes synonymous with impossible demands – and both are hypocritical.

The priest's task

We must then acknowledge frankly that while within the priesthood we encounter examples of great moral courage, we also see examples of lives that are seemingly more marked by sin than by grace. We forget the gallery of sin-streaked priests in the pages of Graham Greene at our peril. Priestly ministry is exercised by those who are so called by God, but who are yet sinners. In the present context this must not be misunderstood; this is not a licence for priests to persist in abuse, in manipulation of others, in the misuse of their privilege. It is, however, a reminder that where God has called a sinner to his service, the community of the Church has a responsibility in pointing up all that is filled with the Spirit and offering support and protection to the weak.

We cannot return to an ordering of the Church in which the priest stood above the laity on a pedestal. We cannot because it encourages distortion in the body of Christ, but also because it obscures the way in which priests can realize their priesthood only to the extent that they are fulfilling their call to life in Christ – and that call can be fulfilled only in company with others, the company above all of those with whom we break bread. Equally we cannot forsake the distinctiveness of the priestly life and allow the service of priesthood to squeeze through the gaps in an otherwise indistinguishable contemporary man or woman's life.

Once we accept this as the context for the discussion it becomes possible to set concerns over sexual morality in the wider concern for a holy, disciplined life. The priest shares the social context of the Church with all the baptized. Every priest shares the temptations and desires that are common to all. The possibility of being a priest to others does not require sinlessness (which is not in any case an option), but a persistent attention to ensure that all the attractions, desires, lusts and temptations are held within the disciplines of holiness. This means not only that we consider them in prayer, that we offer them in the Eucharist, that we acknowledge them in penitence, but that whenever we are moving towards the boundaries of what is generally acceptable we seek greater openness rather than greater privacy. This applies as much to the priest who has become compulsively bound to the weekly lottery as to the priest entangled in a relationship with someone who is married; as much to the priest who lives a significant part of his life within the gay subculture and allows of no interaction with the rest of his life as to the priest who is becoming dependent on alcohol; as much to the priest who persists in a lifeless marriage out of a narrow commitment to the vows, without any awareness of the needs of the partner in the marriage as to the priest who, after two broken marriages, is content to think that the third too may be but a stepping-stone to finding the one, true, lasting relationship.

Life together

If this is the stance of the individual, the Church as a fellowship of believers has another task. The critical tools at our disposal have taken away any lingering suggestion that the Christian moral life is something neatly packaged, clear in its boundaries and unchanging in its structure. We now acknowledge that the early Church did not so much fashion a new morality that could be called 'Christian' as draw together an assembly of practices and values which had been tried and tested elsewhere – and then proceed to 'Christianize' them by the way they were integrated into the life of the Christian community, and by the way in which they tested them against the life, teaching, death and resurrection of Jesus Christ.

Now reflection on the early stages of the formation of a Christian morality is powerfully suggestive of the role of the Church today. Robin Gill has claimed that 'moral behaviour in society is thought to be dependent upon an overspill from religion' and 'Christian values once shaped society, they were the moral values of our society',[8] and to the extent that that is true it is clear that, in a multicultural, multi-faith society there is little point in hoping that the values and practices of the Christian community will be self-evidently right to those outside it. Not only is a distinctive Christian morality now less obvious to those outside the Church, but those who seek to follow Christ find that a distinctive Christian approach has fewer echoes in the general responses and attitudes of society. Further, their moral choices are confused and made more difficult by the sheer range of possible competing arguments and there is no particular encouragement to make a Christian choice. It becomes apparently plausible to live according to Christian standards and traditions within the confines of the Church, and to live according to the current wisdom of the world beyond it. This suggests that the Church, constituted as a community of disciples, will need increasingly to be able to be exactly the kind of community that can call us to fidelity by the persistent return to the gospel; the kind of community that is able to live in, but not of the world. At the same time, there is an urgent need to resist the temptation to a kind of ghetto Christianity.

The combined effect of the loss of the near-universal appeal of Christian moral values and the move to meet the demand for personal authenticity is to underscore the need for a rediscovery of forms of Christian community in which the former can once again be acknowledged, not as external impositions but as integral to the life of faith and the latter can be encountered as gift – fundamentally gift of the Spirit, manifested in the lives and interactions of the members of the community. Such a rediscovery is a necessary antidote to the state of moral *anomia* that threatens to overtake us. It is inimical to the gospel for individuals or groups to claim as rights certain ways of living and behaving while refusing to other members of the community any partic-ipation in the discernment. Confrontations between members of gay rights' movements and the Archbishop of Canterbury will do nothing for anyone. The discovery of Christian moral authenticity belongs within the life of the parish, the diocese and the monastery – and in differing degrees within each grouping. It will always be subject to the absolute standard of the Spirit, to that manifestation of love, joy, peace, gentleness, patience, self-control and the rest that cannot be counterfeited. In such an atmosphere, we are better able to be 'surprised by joy' and to see the presence and grace of Christ in relationships that had before only called forth condemnation from us; but we are also better able to appeal to one another for constant conversion and repentance. So too we shall be better equipped to live in the present when there is little hope of a broad-based consensus on the central questions, but a desperate need for us all to be able to learn from one another and appreciate the insights of those with whom we disagree fundamentally.

When all is said and done, at a time of crisis for the ordained ministry, when the sexual history of so many priests has been troubling to them and embarrassing, if not offensive, to others, it is right to remind our-selves of the nature of the call on which priesthood is founded. Priests are called before and beyond all else to love and serve the flock and to lay down their lives for the sheep. This strangely persisting, pastoral image of the priesthood returns us to the Good Shepherd and sets us before the One to whom we shall give account for the faith that is in us.

Further reading

Davies, J. and G. Loughlin (eds.), *Sex These Days*, Sheffield Academic Press, 1997.

Gill, R., *Moral Communities*, Exeter: University of Exeter Press, 1992.

Hefling, C. (ed.), *Our Selves, Our Souls and Bodies*, Cambridge, Mass.: Cowley, 1984.

MacIntyre, A., *After Virtue*, Duckworth, 1981.

MacIntyre, A., *Whose Justice, Which Rationality?* London: Duckworth, 1988.

MacIntyre, A., *Three Rival Versions of Moral Enquiry*, Notre Dame, 1991.

Mason, K., *Priesthood and Society*, Norwich: Canterbury Press, 1992.

Taylor, C., *Sources of the Self: The Making of the Modern Identity*, Cambridge University Press, 1989.

Thatcher, A., *Liberating Sex*, London: SPCK, 1993.

For all Christians, belief in our high
calling has to be sustained in the face of
frailties inherent in individuals, society and
the Church. This challenge is increased by
the fruitful tension between the priesthood
of all the baptized and the calling of some
to be priests among them. This calling is
only sustainable if rooted and grounded
in God, for however varied our circle of
family and friends, and however great the
hurly-burly of the Christian community
and its ministry, the priest's position is a
lonely one ...

9
Detachment in Priesthood and Community

BENJAMIN GORDON-TAYLOR

The title of this chapter might imply an excursion into former notions of priestly 'separateness'. A view of the Church rooted in the baptismal vocation of the whole people could easily and unnecessarily do away with a fruitful dimension of 'detachment' in the life of the priest. As a baptized and ordained person, the priest exists in sacramental relationship with the community, and ought neither physically nor spiritually to be separate from it in ways that suggest *non*-attachment to everyday life and the theological and social issues that attend it. Nevertheless, there are important senses in which priests can only be free to engage by also being prepared to *dis*-engage.

Getting alongside

In recent years, many have asserted that the role of the Church is to 'get alongside', and to 'be with people where they are'. While both phrases have become pastoral clichés, their meaning is clear. The task of the Church is to minister to the community by reaching out to it as it actually is, rather than passively expecting a sudden active Christian commitment from people before anything else can be done. 'Being with people where they are' is about making the incarnation known in the community. The starting point is the conviction that Jesus is already present in it, however uninterested in 'religion' it may appear. This understanding does not seek to justify itself by quantifiable 'results', but places the emphasis on the very *doing* of the pastoral task in faith as an active interpretation of the gospel, seeing any discernible fruits as a privileged gift of God. The gift is welcome, but is not the sole justification for the task. We do not minister to the bereaved because we hope to get them to come to church, but because they have a pastoral need. If they do come to church as a result of the care given, then that is cause for thanksgiving because they have experienced Jesus for themselves and are actively seeking to know him. It is not an evangelistic feather in the cap for the local church.

The pastoral task ought not to mean that those to whom the Church reaches out are swamped by an excess of heavy evangelism, pastoral zeal or social theory with a religious tinge, but are approached and received mindful of God's image in them, with equal respect, openness and charity. In maritime terminology, a ship that is 'alongside' is beside the quay, supporting itself in the water but linked to the quay for the purpose of reloading, fuelling, maintenance and exchange of personnel. Ship and quay retain their independence, and yet are mutually interdependent both when physically linked and when far apart. In pastoral relationships, the starting point of ministry is a fundamental acceptance of human autonomy and the need for consent that acknowledges elements of both dependence and detachment. An element of detachment is present even in the most involved and delicate situations. The one ministering to a person can never be that person, but can minister to them both in their presence (listening, conversation, practical and sacramental help) and when physically detached from them (prayer, separate action on their behalf, and consideration of their needs and of the possible solutions at greater length than is possible when in direct contact). There is a place for both, but there is no blueprint describing their precise balance. Pastoral ministry can never be defined by certainty, or carried out with a book of instructions; it is carried out in faith, aided by experience, and defined by mystery, by what is unknown rather than known. The work of Christ in another person's life is not necessarily going to be on public display, and certainly nobody has an automatic right to see it. They have instead to trust that he is present, and cooperate with him in reconciling and healing, without necessarily ever seeing his face or feeling his touch, except in the faces, through the hands, and in the words and actions of those on both sides of the pastoral relationship.

The pastoral task is not the preserve of ordained specialists, but belongs to the whole Church. Those not ordained may very well be more experienced and instinctively better at knowing what balance is required, and in possession of a greater confidence in the mystery of Christ's love, which lies at the heart of the task. The role of priests is not to dominate the task but to lead and focus it for the whole people. In doing so, and in being vulnerable exemplars of the Church's care for all, they can experience and be aware of elements of hiddenness and detachment in the community, in their own lives and in the practice of their priesthood which can actually assist them in this complex work of pastoral leadership, and ensure that the people of God are inspired and fed for the task which has been entrusted to them all through their baptism.

The hiddenness of the community

Pastoral effectiveness can be judged less by the amount of time a priest spends in the company of parishioners than by the quality of the pastoral relationship formed between the local church and the community as a whole, a quality measured by the criteria suggested in the previous section. It is a sacramental relationship arising from the gift of the Spirit given at ordination, the Spirit-led consent of the local church and the tacit, largely unarticulated consent of the community. It is not defined or justified only by visible engagement or frenetic activity, but also by elements that are hidden from view. However much priests visit, go to pubs and walk the streets, their knowledge of the community will be limited by closed doors, private lives, and the infinite possibilities of human existence. As the priest in Graham Greene's novel *The Heart of the Matter* says, 'The Church knows all the rules. But it doesn't know what goes on in a single human heart.'[1] This may not be entirely true in a parish where the pastoral relationship is in good health, but it does remind us that everything priests know about the community individually and corporately is privilege and gift, and never a right. They live with being able to see only what it is given them to see, and indeed often what people want them to see. But ordained ministers are concerned not only with what they can see, but also equally with what is not visible, the much larger hidden dimension that they hold in prayer and trust.

There is a constant awareness that there is always more, an awareness that can only be met with humility. The community itself will therefore always remain largely detached from the priest, but this limitation in the priest's vision does not need to be a source of discouragement or lead to a sense of failure. Rather can it be seen as a positive defining factor of priestly ministry in the parish. That there is always more to know about the community does not necessarily indicate the priest's irrelevance or idleness. It mirrors our relationship with God whose depths we enter but whose limits we never find, and also points within us to our own hidden selves, which we have not fully exposed or mapped. Christian priests are themselves part of the hiddenness and detachment of the community, because they themselves are human and made in God's image. Not knowing, and admitting to it, are healthy reminders that we are dealing with a God and a humanity that no strategy or model, no amount of busyness, liturgical perfection or evangelistic outreach will wholly succeed in boxing up or categorizing. If these things work well, they reveal the distance yet to be travelled, not the chequered flag. This is the reality of a priest's ministry exercised in this messy, mysterious but wonderful and life-affirming context, a ministry that itself has hidden depths that feed its effectiveness and stability.

The hiddenness of the priest

If the priest's view of the community is constrained by these factors, the community's view of the priest will be limited by the fact that priests exist in small numbers and are not the sole object of attention. They may only prompt a glimmer of awareness, and that formed by television stereotypes and tabloid sensations. To many, perhaps most people in the community, the priest's existence is of little or no day-to-day significance. They have more important things to do than worry about what the parish priest is doing and why. The first aspect of priestly detachment is therefore an entirely practical one. But there are other ways in which detachment forms part of priests' lives, ways directly and positively connected with their relationship with the largely hidden community they are called to serve.

Engagement with people needs preparation. Pastoral relationships should not be characterized by aloofness, implied superiority or misplaced monkishness, but by openness, communication and trust, qualities that need nurture and development. In 'getting alongside' the people of the community, the priest casts out lines of encouragement and opportunity, while lines of hope, need and sometimes desperation are thrown back in return. Priests need the confidence, stability and judgement to deal with these possibilities, and to know when to be reactive and when proactive. The right kind of detachment is an essential part of this, and is naturally expected by people.

Priests and hermits

In its Christian form, in its antecedents in Greek antiquity and its contemporary parallels in other faiths, the solitary or hermit tradition can help us understand how detachment is a fruitful part of the life of the priest, and lead to a more fruitful ministry at the heart of the community. A common thread running through the tradition is that hermits, while they have chosen physically to separate themselves from society, retain vibrant links with everyday life. This can be both in terms of their life of contemplation and intercession, holding the world before God, and as a result of the perceptions of others who seek them out for advice about everyday dilemmas and concerns. As Peter France says of a hermit who had once lived near his home in Greece:

> His disruptive popularity had been the consequence of his giving sound advice. And that advice had little to do with the spiritual path he was following. The problems these women carried to him with his Friday provisions had to do with their relations with husbands and children, their sick animals, their quarrels with neighbours, the choice of husbands for their daughters. They brought their sexual tensions and the anxieties of married and family life to a monk committed to

lifelong chastity and solitude. They asked advice on the many problems of living together in society from somebody who had chosen to live outside it.[2]

The two areas of this solitary life – contemplation and the need to give seemingly unrelated advice – can be applied to the very public life of the priest, both as one who is approached by others and one who is to do the approaching. Both are grounded in detachment.

Paradoxically, in the hermit tradition, people who appear to live outside the normal structures of society are approached as experts on that very society, able to give counsel on matters they are not directly involved in. Yet their detachment can give them a different perspective, and an ability to see situations in a more balanced way than the people actually embroiled in them. They are, perhaps, adept at what has been described as: 'Seeing life whole ... including those parts of it which have been characterised ... as poetic, parabolic, intuitive and contemplative'.[3] This has strong parallels with the priest's role as one called to exercise a ministry of balanced vision in the parish as pastoral leader of the community, spiritual guide, listener, and with the explicit addition of the guaranteed confidentiality that is an extension of the traditional seal of the confessional. It is a role that depends on a certain restlessness and fluidity, and a resistance to definition and model:

> The priest, paradoxically, is both engaged and dis-engaged from life: an inhabiter of margins, a dweller of the verges of the mass of experience, at least in the minds of many of those he meets; yet perhaps because of that very dislocation is able to see the whole ... wandering himself, he is used to discerning signs in the topography of the lives of those who either frequently or momentarily find themselves before him, seeking direction.[4]

For these reasons, there is (or ought to be) a strong perception in parishes that the priest is available to be consulted, both in the first place and when other potential sources of help have proved fruitless or have betrayed trust:

> The Parish Eucharist had just finished, and most people had left the church. As he returned to the vestry after chatting with parishioners, the priest noticed a couple still sitting in the pews. He hadn't seen them before, and went up to introduce himself. Shaking hands with him, they looked a little embarrassed. 'I wonder if we could talk to you for a minute or

two?' said the man. 'Of course, how can I help?' the priest replied. Looking nervously at his wife, the man continued, 'Well, we have been having problems in our family, and we just don't know where to turn. In a small town like this, everyone seems to know everyone else. We've found that if we confide in some people, they go and tell other people about our private business. We were getting desperate, but then we thought, perhaps a priest could help. If we tell you, you won't tell anyone else, will you?'[5]

In this typical example, the priest's detachment makes possible a ministry to people who have been let down by those in their community who participate in potentially harmful gossip. The priest is not a participant in the network of whispers that can be a feature of a small town or other close community. Impartiality is often expected of priests, but it is not always the correct stance. It can be very damaging when a priest is seen to ally with a particular section of the community over against another. When the vulnerability of the margins is abandoned for the apparent safety of a social stockade, credibility and trust can soon be absent, and the reconciler can become either a combatant or an ostrich with head in the sand. Either way, irreparable harm can be done to the pastoral relationship with the community. This is not detachment, but separation. In certain circumstances, however, the justice of the gospel may require priests to put their heads above the parapet in defence of victims – this is not abandoning vulnerability, but embracing it all the more. The margin in this case is that inhabited by those rejected by society through exploitation, prejudice and lack of compassion. The priest is both free and called to go there, just as Jesus was and did, through the detachment which is part and parcel of priesthood, if necessary cutting across social convention and the prevailing mood in order to reach those left stranded by these things. The detachment in the priest identifies with the detachment of those who don't fit in, except that the priest's role is to reconcile them with society and with God, not drive them still further over the edge.

Although resistant to definition and label, then, priests are a part of the community with a perceived role characterized by unconditional openness, a willingness to listen, and implicit trust. Those who do not attend church and who would not necessarily say that they have an explicit Christian faith can be drawn to the priest because of these characteristics of the priestly ministry. Their need comes alongside the priest's pastoral concern, and the lines of love that held Christ to the cross are fastened and allowed to do their work. The priest cannot have this role without detachment and self-realism. The rope of compassion is woven in the priest's life by the meditation and prayer in which the priest's own vulnerability and brokenness are confronted, and out of which the ministry of reconciliation in its broadest sense is empowered by personal experience of cross and resurrection. The priest is able to be the quay because he has also been the ship, tossed and turned by the storms of the same temptation, suffering, betrayal and sheer loss of nerve that assail every human being:

> *Then he spoke, and a stormy wind arose,*
> *   which tossed high the waves of the sea.*
> *They mounted up to the heavens and fell back to the depths;*
> *   their hearts melted because of their peril.*
> *They reeled and staggered like drunkards*
> *   and were at their wits' end.*
> *Then they cried to the Lord in their trouble,*
> *   and he delivered them from their distress.*
> *He stilled the storm to a whisper*
> *   and quieted the waves of the sea.*
> *Then they were glad because of the calm,*
> *   and he brought them to the harbour they were bound for.*[6]

Praying alone: seen and unseen

The couple in the anecdote sought out the priest in a place which they associated with his ministry: the church building. It is assumed that a priest will be found in a church, and there is little or no questioning of the connection between person and place. It is a natural assumption, not needing to be justified in the minds of people in the community, even if their attitude towards a priest is one of hostility. In this country, priests do not in fact sit in church all day waiting for pastoral encounters, although there may be advertised times apart from services when, for example, 'a priest is available for counsel and/or confession'. In many churches in Paris, however, there is a small room with a glass door, in which at most times of the day a priest can be seen sitting vested in alb and purple stole, visible and available to all who come through the door. The sacramental person waits, inviting the animation of the sacramental relationship between priest and community, the one 'chosen out of the people' in order to be for that people a sign and focus of God's gifts of love, given to all.

If it is not a contradiction in terms, there is a public loneliness about the figure of the priest in church which points to and shares in the loneliness which gnaws at the heart of every human being, the loneliness which Jesus knew in Gethsemane and which was the occasion of his resolve to do the Father's will. The church building can be the priest's

Gethsemane; self-doubt is confronted where it cannot be avoided, in the silence of a heart directed to God. There is nowhere to run for cover, in spite of the apparent security of 'my stall', the favourite spiritual works lined up in the prie-dieu, the well-thumbed office-book. Very often the church, and not the streets of the parish, is the desert where priests confront their demons, where others often come to be freed from theirs, and where the spiritual realities of the life and the task are illuminated by the glare of God's love. But although the priest may be alone, the activity of prayer is accountable to the community in the midst of which it is happening. The cost of the undeniable privilege of having free access to and responsibility for a place hallowed by the prayers of others is the surrendering of spiritual anonymity, in order that very often through the priest's own frailty and brokenness a ministry of intercession and reconciliation is exercised at the centre of the community. This the priest does in physical and architectural detachment, but with the purpose of growing ever more deeply attached and available to those for whom it is done.

Praying alone is not a sign of irrelevance, but part of the reality of engagement with the mystery of God present to us in our daily lives. The detachment and vulnerability of the priest praying alone in church, a public person in a public building, mirrors the detachment and vulnerability that accompany pastoral ministry among and alongside the members of the community. It is a sign of Christ's willingness to set himself apart in order that others may be reconciled to one another and to the Father. It is a ministry of service that demands not a detachment of personality or manner, but of the heart and of the soul; a belief that 'faith is the assurance of things hoped for, the conviction of things not seen' (Heb. 11.1, RSV). If priests believe that the Spirit of God is at work in their ministry, whatever form it takes, they must acknowledge that it also works within them: in order to reconcile others, they must be reconciled themselves.

Being alone

There can be a difference between loneliness and being alone. Loneliness occurs through natural circumstance or as a result of something amiss in lifestyle or relationships. It is therefore essentially negative, and in the life of a priest it can be mentally and spiritually crippling. It is fine as an image, as we have just suggested, but if it becomes an overbearing personal reality it can bring to the priest's life a kind of detachment that is definitely not fruitful and may be damaging to priest and community. It can occur if the priest forgets the human dimension of priesthood, that it is because of humanity and not in spite of it that Christ died and that ministry is exercised in his name. It is because we as God's creatures are utterly loveable that God takes the undeniable risk of enabling us to minister to one another. Indeed, we can get so taken with this that we forget that we have a responsibility of care towards ourselves. When a priest allows the ceaseless pressures of pastoral ministry to exclude time for physical, mental and spiritual renewal, humanity is often excluded as well. Henri Nouwen describes the figure of the lonely priest:

> The paradox is that he who has been taught to love everyone in reality finds himself without any friends; that he who trained himself in mental prayer often is not able to be alone with himself. Having opened himself to every outsider, there is no room left for the insider. The walls of the intimate enclosure of his privacy crumble, and there is no place left to be with himself. The priest who has given away so much of himself creates an inexhaustible need to be constantly with others in order to feel that he is a whole person.[7]

Such loneliness arises from good intentions, but also from a lack of confidence in the need to be detached from practical pastoral tasks both for spiritual renewal and for pursuing activities and interests that feed the whole human person and that, if applicable, nurture the 'domestic church' of the family. The latter is a particular concern for married clergy. It is equally important, however, for the priest to 'be alone' with the self. To be so is largely a matter of positive choice and active self-discipline, but also founded on the knowledge that Christ is present in the solitude.

The priest as contemplative

There are dangers in drawing excessively close parallels between the secular life of the parish priest and the religious life of monastic communities. There can be a temptation to model pastoral priesthood on a perceived spiritual fulfilment of the monk, when in fact this can amount to a retreat from the community the priest is supposed to serve, and can suggest the models of spiritual caste applied to priesthood before the rebalanced vision of the Church evolved in the last 30 years. It would also be to misunderstand the life of religious orders in the contemporary Church. However, the monastic elements of common life and stability can speak usefully to the priest in a busy parish, and in their contemplative form can illuminate the theme of detachment with which we are concerned.

The spiritual life of the priest has been a rich vein of exploration in the past, and has prompted many books and manuals. But our renewed vision of the Church as founded on baptism should lead us to seek an integrated spirituality of the whole parish community that takes account of those on its margins as well as those who have made an explicit commitment to the church. The priest's task is to facilitate the formation of such a common spirituality, and to seek such nourishment for the self as feeds this specific role as well as the life of the baptized Christian, which the priest also is. In this, the priest relies on the ministry of vision, the willingness to see the bigger picture, to have and to nurture in others the overarching sense of God's loving activity in the world that serves so powerfully at the pastoral heart of priestly service. The priest's spiritual life, like the life of the monk, must be one of stability – seeing life whole, despite the antagonisms and petty frustrations that can seem to dominate parish (and community) life. The priest's spiritual journey, like that of any human being, ought to reflect the double-edged nature of our engagement with God: to 'be still and know', and yet at the same time to 'press on to know the Lord'. Pastoral action, pressing on to know the Lord in the lives of those the priest serves and to make him known in those same lives, must be balanced by a contemplation of the God who embraces us as we are and where we are, holding all souls in life and, to paraphrase Irenaeus, showing forth his glory in the living human being in order that the life of humanity might be the vision of God.[8]

Contemplation itself has a double aspect. It is a solitary activity, in which God and the human soul gaze with utter fascination at one another in the purest way that is possible this side of eternity, and yet it is a participation in the life of the whole Church, militant, expectant and triumphant, an immersion in the wonderfully crowded life of heaven that continually spills over into our everyday existence. In this it is closely related to the Eucharist, itself an objective participation in the mystery of God that makes present the reality of Christ's saving love. Liturgy and spirituality are not really separate, in the sense that both delight in the transformation of the ordinary stuff of creation. The priest contemplates, experiences and facilitates this transformation liturgically and pastorally. It is the privilege of a ministry that 'involves many transformations; a passage from matter to form, from mere potential to actuality, from disorder to order, from the broken to the healed, from the fragmented to the whole'.[9] This possibility of transformation the priest must know alone with God, in the deepest self, in order that it may be known in others through the ministry of transformation to which the priest is called.

The gospel does not give easy answers on great questions, but offers a two-eyed vision often found in contrasting statements. The priest (originally the bishop, but then, by delegation, the presbyter) is in this fashion a point where many crossing threads come together and are held (not only by the priest's hand) at a focus . . .

10
The Priest as Focus

GEORGE GUIVER CR

It is a children's service. Each child present has brought a torch. One by one they shine their torch on a small picture set high up on the wall in the darkness of the roof. It is a sunny day, so the effect of each torch in turn is dim. Then all are asked to shine their torches simultaneously. The difference is dramatic – there now seems to be a powerful spotlight: the picture radiates in a pool of white light. I have sometimes used that as an illustration for talking about the body of Christ, showing that we can't be Christians in privacy or on our own private terms – we need each other in order to see, and to help each other to see.

The priest at the vortex

The picture of converging beams of light is also an image of the life of the priest, who is a focus of the entire life of the parish, standing at the centre of many converging lines. This can be felt at its strongest when problems arise. Various people raise a problem about, say, the distribution of responsibilities for the annual fete. For each of them the problem may be a source of anxiety or anger, but it will only be one element in their life. They can go away and totally forget about it until the next meeting. Their part in it has the strength and energy of one small torch. The feelings of all these people, however, converge on the priest, who can be taken aback and have sleepless nights, a sense of being let down, and even feel oppressed by an enormous and insupportable weight. The priest cannot so easily pass on from it to other things until the next occasion. Not only have the chorus of dim little lights converged on this person in a powerful way, but there can be a tendency to further magnification because of the special way the priest depends on the parish. For most other people parish affairs might be important, but they do have other concerns as well, and will spend most of their time attending to them. For their vicar on the other hand it is everything, and on it hangs not just livelihood, but even sense of self.

For the single priest, but also for the married one, the parish is a kind of spouse. There is a sense of 'marriage' to the parish, which holds not only at the personal level, but also has to do with the priest's relationship to the gospel. It can be easy to be discouraged – what after all is the point of struggling to help people follow Christ if all they can get worked up about is the parish fete? The storms in parish teacups become hurricanes in the vicarage. On the one hand is a priest who is deeply affected by something in the parish, and on the other a community blissfully unaware of the effect such things can have. Unaware too of how an angry word over the telephone might have just been preceded by angry words from others, or problems from another area of parish life. Little glimmers of tension from different directions build up into a powerful effect on their target.

Anyone entering upon ordained ministry becomes aware of living at a point of focus, and they need to understand the way this convergence on the priest operates, in order to make sense of it and not be debilitated by it. One danger is to take everything personally: largeness of mind is needed which not only keeps it all in proportion, but is also ready to see things to be learnt, and growing to be done, in the process of these conflicts. The priest has to be big enough to handle it, and to some degree or other suffer it, without taking things personally. Obvious words that come to mind are resilience, patience, humility, sensitivity, the very things we probably haven't got! Sensitivity to others is a sign of being bound to them, something fundamental to Christian community and roles within it. When a candidate makes profession in a religious community, the community may say: 'As you have bound yourself to us, so we bind ourselves to you.' Being bound to others means exposing myself to them, and realizing that they have exposed themselves to me and what I might wreak upon them. For the priest this carries a cost, which is always there, lurking round the next corner.

Resilience and a sense of proportion are a great help, but they are not enough on their own, and can even get in the way of the priestly task: part of that task is to face the darknesses of other people and to take into oneself their effects. Everything that happens in the parish is there to turn the priest to God. All of it is God at work, part of the process of our conversion. The priest who is less affected by life will not get far below the surface of pastoral ministry. On the other hand, becoming too weighed down by its problems can reveal a different kind of superficiality: If 'my grace is sufficient for you', then the potential discouragements may bring the priest teetering near the edge of giving up, but faithfulness in prayer and centring the whole life on God will prevent it happening.

God can be edged out of a priest's ministry in a variety of ways. It might be a given fact of the priest's theology – the transcendent God has disappeared from the priest's horizon. When that happens, difficulties are bound to be expected, or else they will be coped with by filling the hole with other ideologies and activities from the 'secular' world. Among clergy such as those of the 'Sea of Faith' movement this abandonment of God can be candidly acknowledged, and then the foundation for exercise of priesthood becomes simply the structural, financial and organizational basis provided by the Church in a way in which no other organization provides it. There are many more clergy, however, who live in a way in which God has been sidelined, without fully admitting it to themselves. Many clergy sideline God unintentionally through drift and neglect. Often where a priest is weighed down by the problems of Christian ministry, or feels a sense of being burnt out, this would never have happened if God had been allowed to be at the centre. Turning to God in penitence and prayer, with petition and intercession, rooted in the Scriptures and the sacraments, is the essential foundation of all pastoral ministry.

A priest may feel the burden of pastoral office, and may smart at points where it pinches, but the God-centred priest will know that it doesn't stop there, it goes on to God. God is in it, and at work in it, it is all sacramental, even when everything seems to be at its worst. The life of the priest is one undivided whole, in which every single thing, profound or trivial, is offered with Christ to the Father, in a priestly offering. Every waking and sleeping moment is one reality, without gaps, interruptions or intermissions. Resilience is a great help, but is not enough. Everything that happens has to turn the priest to God, and that means seeing God in everything, turning to God in everything. In such statements many people think of God in isolation as a figment in the mind, and they struggle with it. The only God, however, who can carry the faithful priest through the vicissitudes of a lifetime's ministry, is the God who is incarnate in the body of Christ, its outward manifestations and sacramental life. In other words, this priest's ministry is grounded in a sense of the Church.

Not less than everything

Such a total vision of the priest's life is pointed to in the New Testament, where we are told that Christ asks not less than everything: he asks for total commitment. 'No one who puts a hand to the plough and looks back is fit for the kingdom of God' (Luke 9.62, NRSV). Sayings like that make us feel uncomfortable, for we have holidays in Ibiza, evenings at the pub, the odd day out on the razzle. Ananias and Sapphira were struck dead at the apostles' feet for having tried to keep a little back from what is given to God. 'No one who looks back is fit for the kingdom of God.' That is not the sort of thing we like to think while chewing candyfloss on Morecambe Pier. Most clergy lead a relatively normal life in the midst of modern Western society. We live like everybody else, not a life with nowhere to lay our head. We don't abandon father and mother, we don't decide to hate them, to refuse to bury our relatives after their death.

Apart from that, there is another problem. Total commitment can get out of hand, leading to loony sects and exclusive cults. We find problems with it not only there, but also in the heart of the Church. The life of religious communities in more recent centuries was often just like this. Monks and nuns could be treated pitilessly by their superiors, in a process reducing the individual to unquestioning obedience and self-abnegation, something that was seen as following the absolute commands of the Lord. Or we might think of some strict and austere forms of Christianity and the destructive effects of their narrowness. We have a problem with these sayings of Jesus not only because they seem to ask too much, but also because they can easily be corrupted into a faith which is doctrinaire, pitiless, obsessed with lack of self-worth and keen to correct people and tell them what they should be doing.

There is a story about St Antony of Egypt on this theme. Antony was renowned for his holiness and austerity, so it was a slight shock for a passer-by to see the venerable hermit and some monks relaxing and enjoying themselves. Antony said to the visitor, 'Put an arrow in your bow and shoot it.' So he did. And the old man said, 'Shoot again a bit further', and he did so. Then the old man said, 'Shoot yet again, further still.' And the hunter replied, 'If I bend my bow so much I will break it.' Then Anthony said to him, 'It is the same with the work of God. If we stretch the brothers beyond measure, they will soon break. Sometimes it is necessary to come down to meet our needs.' This strikes us as wise and sensible, but how do we square enjoying ourselves with the gospel call to total self-sacrifice? One thing Antony is not intending to say is that we can have a rest from the gospel. If a wayfarer comes up to us in the street, or if we are angry with a shop assistant because of some problem, the temptation is to behave as if no one saw us. I can shun this old man or be angry with this shop assistant because no one will know I am a Christian, no one will know I am a priest. When that happens we are taking a rest from the gospel, something a Christian cannot do.

The other mistake is to fail to rest at all, to fail to rest within the gospel. We can be like Antony's passer-by, so intent on serious following of Christ as to suppress our humanity. As we chew our candyfloss on the pier, as we peer at what the butler saw or just lean over the side holding a fishing rod, we are still living the gospel, following the plough. We cannot have a rest from the gospel – all of it is a living of the gospel. If when I'm on holiday I can't think about the Lord's call, then I have misunderstood the call.

On the other hand, if I reject innocent pleasures, and decide the gospel is too important for self-indulgence, if I become weighed down with the burden of the gospel life, and never let my hair down as a flesh-and-blood human being, then I have still misunderstood the call. The New

Testament itself shows us the way. Paul encourages people to take a drop of wine. The Lord tells the disciples to come apart and rest a while. When the risen Lord meets the disciples returning from fishing, he provides the most obvious thing their humanity needs – a cooked breakfast. Christ's approach to people is holistic – calling to obedience, but to a holistic obedience, not a relentless one.

There is more. We need to be able not only to relax, but even to be fools. There is a little book written in the sixteenth century by Erasmus, which he called *In Praise of Folly*. In it Erasmus praises foolishness, silliness and folly as underrated virtues. He even says that anyone who is perfectly serious and sensible cannot live. 'Why', he says, 'do we kiss and cuddle little children, if not because they are still so delightfully foolish?' 'If a wise man', he then goes on, 'wishes to become a father, there is no way to that end except by playing the fool.' In telling these truths Erasmus is like the child in the story of the king with no clothes. He is disturbingly honest about people as they really are, rather than as we would like them to be. 'Go to church,' he says. 'If the priest deals with serious subjects the whole congregation is dozing, yawning, feeling bored. But when he begins to tell some cock-and-bull story, they awake, sit up and hang upon his lips.'

And we might well comment: 'Look at the preaching of Jesus.' He was a past master at bringing people to God through cock-and-bull stories – camels and needles' eyes, burglars, dishonest managers, foolish brides-maids, and a long, gaudy procession of foolish/wise humanity. God has chosen the foolish things of the world to shame the wise. In the topsy-turvy world of the gospel wisdom is folly, and folly wisdom. True serious-ness cannot be found without a sense of humour. However difficult or serious a situation may be, the priest needs a ready sense of humour, and the ability to laugh at self and others. And perhaps just as the spirit of prayer is cultivated by the daily office, so the sense of humour is fed by relaxation, holidays and 'foolishness'.

If the whole of life is a living of the gospel, then even eating candyfloss on the pier is, but it is done truly foolishly, truly giving ourselves to the harmless delights of life, and not crippling them with some earnest veneer; everything that happens each day in the priest's life is part of the sacrament of the priestly life. Christ's is a call to bring with us the whole of ourselves, and not to forget that we are human; for all of that humanity is to be redeemed, not just the more serious bits of it.

As well as the essential role of a sense of humour, there is something else that needs to be part of the priest's equipment: that ancient insight of the Christian tradition called 'discretion'. Discretion as a technical term is partly about right balance, a moderate and wise weighing of all things, not in a worldly sense, but with Christ as its agent. Discretion means a tempering of idealism with a recognition of our humanity. Overwork, over-pastoring of those in need, taking on too much, sacrificing rest and recreation to the supposed needs of the gospel, are all instances of lack of discretion. Discretion, however, is not a matter of damping everything down into a boring equilibrium. It could well mean a call to 'work hard and play hard'.

If wisdom inclines us to avoid the trap of inhuman relentlessness, it also warns us against the opposite temptation of simply awarding ourselves an easy life, following Christ in doses, but avoiding over-stretching ourselves. Walter Frere, in speaking to the Community of the Resurrection, once described this problem as 'the mere achievement of various sorts and degrees of individual usefulness, but no community – much; no poverty – much; no obedience – much'. Between that and the opposite extreme of being God-avoiding workaholics there stands a mean that is higher than both – a giving of absolutely everything to God. The paradoxical thing is that this is a middle way that asks nothing less than everything, but this 'everything' refers to a life lived to the full, in work and in play. It is not a sacrificing of our capacity to live life to the full, but the greatest realization of it. Christians are those who believe in fullness of life, and the priestly calling is one of holding fullness of life before people's eyes. That cannot be done if we do not know fullness of life ourselves.

The priest as the outsider

Standing at the heart of things can at the same time make you an outsider. One of the most difficult things is in trying to see how the two dimensions relate: being integral to the Christian community, and being set apart. The priest is an outsider in representing to the local church the larger world of the Church universal. Parish life needs to be seen from a different perspective than that of the parish pump. Most members of a congregation do this in a variety of ways, but the priest is specifically equipped and authorized to do it in basic areas, such as theology, pastoral care and worship. This is often confused with exercise of power, and too often that is how it is practised. In one parish a priest in cooperation with the people builds up an effective catechumenate programme. A new priest is then installed who dismantles it all – a petty dictator marches in and devastates the ecology. In another parish the approach is more subtle, but under the cloak of a high doctrine of lay ministry there ferments in the vicar an exasperation with people's apathy and apparent inability to commit themselves to much. Every profession has its *mores* and its culture, but there are times and places where the clerical culture has become so distinctive (and aware of it) as to become a kind of freemasonry. True priestly authority rests not on power, nor on us-and-them attitudes, but on community and its commission from God.

If the priest is to be imbued with what is 'outside' the community, as well as what is 'inside', then those who follow this calling will change as they enter upon it. Changes need to take place at the level of personal formation if the role is to mean anything. It is instructive here to look at the recent trend to ordain older candidates. The Church has benefited from a wealth of experience that has been brought to bear by them. There is a downside to this, however. The first major job you commit yourself to in life sets your horizons. It establishes ways of identifying priorities, ways of assessing situations, it sets your assumptions about goals, aims and objectives. It sets the horizons within which you operate: it gives you the spectacles with which you see the world. Older candidates for priesthood have to discover that this has to be broken open, questioned at the roots, and left to grow together again in a new way. With some older candidates, however, that does not happen. The horizons remain what they were, and there is a failure to grow into the role of the priest. Limits and habits have become too established, and the person is no longer able to see beyond them. There can be an inability to see the radical demands of the gospel for the challenge that they are. There can be too much faith in skills the world has provided, leaving the person incapable of seeing the degree to which all that is questioned at the root by the sovereignty of God.

The horizons in which the priest operates, however, are also in their own way a limitation. Ordination brings a different vision on things, but new blind spots. Being an outsider means there are ways in which it will never be possible again to be at people's level. Priests are often surprised and discouraged by their congregations, and this problem can be of their own making, because they no longer think like their people. They have to be aware of the drawbacks of their special role.

There is a difficult area here: the priest is also an outsider by living in the view of a public which expects to see an exemplary life. 'The priest,' said John Chrysostom, 'lives in a house made of glass.' The priest is focus of an attention that is often warped by double standards. Many expect clergy to be surrogates for Christian commit-ment and perfection, while the fact that a priest might be a human person with human needs, struggling in an exposed position, does not occur to them. Some folk may expect clergy to lead perfect lives, to be without feelings, fair game for criticism, but at the same time set apart in an awesome way to live out by proxy the 'full' Christian calling. Their instinct is right where it sees the priest as called to focus all that is good in the community, bringing its life in the gospel to a focus in a Christian life. But the priest can only do that with the people: not instead of them nor above them, but in partnership.

Partnership

It is impossible to understand the notion 'mother', or even to call it a notion, without taking into account those people without whom no one can be a mother. 'Motherhood' immediately speaks of relationship and belonging, and so does priesthood. In normal circumstances motherhood connotes more: a total belonging, given away for life to certain others. Only someone who is conscious of this is equipped for the task. Even though in some cases this picture does not hold true for psychological or other reasons, our understanding of motherhood would be seriously impaired if we took it for granted that motherhood does not need a total self-giving. It is perfectly possible for people to grow up as happy and healthy human beings without having had that kind of mothering, but the exception only demonstrates the rule. A person who fulfils this role has to give her whole life to it. Children of course grow up, but at the crucial time a total giving is what we would want and expect.

When it comes to leadership of the Christian family, something similar operates. There are models of ministry that see it in professional terms, reckoning that it is entirely possible later on to change over to another line of work. If, however, you hold the view of Christian calling portrayed in the gospels and implied by the incarnation, then you have a different picture. The gospel call is total. There are elements in it whose 'drastic-ness' takes our breath away: the incarnation, the leaving of everything, the crucifixion. The gospel is drastic, bloody, visceral, shocking.

The Church has a commission to carry that forward. Sometimes it fails, losing touch with the guts and becoming reasonable, measured and manageable in all things. A Church like that can then conceive of a ministry where many or all could have a go at being pastors of the flock, and none would feel bound to it for life. The drastic element in the gospels, however, leads us to expect that some persons will be drastically taken up, and the New Testament points especially to those who are to be shepherds of the flock. In a Church worth its salt some persons will be taken up in this way. Leadership which is not a total offering for life can only fall short of what we understand to be the gospel life for the Church. Yes, there will be other members of the people of God who live out the highest ideals of self-giving, there will be heroism of every kind, self-sacrificing service and at times martyrdom. Those can never be planned for – they arise. But because the gospel is incarnational the Church will also have a drastic note written into its genes, something part of its fingerprints. God calls some to be commissioned, set aside for life in a total, irreversible handover which will be a visible, living planting of the drastic edge of the gospel in the midst of God's people.

This life will not necessarily *feel* drastic, and those who live it can never claim such a heroic role for themselves as individuals. But they are bound to say it about the office. If, as more and more people in the churches are now saying, the Eucharist stands at the heart of the life of the people of God, then this identifying of certain persons by God will be particularly visible in the Eucharist. There we, the people, offer with Christ, we elide our offering of ourselves into the larger generous movement of Christ himself. There in the eucharistic drama the priest is in the Christ-role, which is a continuation of how people expect to see Christ in the priest in the daily round. The priest is the representative person of the call to everyone to be given to God. In responding to a call to drastic giving-up for the whole of life and beyond, in a way which is public and sacramentally sealed, the priest is by tradition the person to preside at the table. Making eucharistic presidency something anyone can have a go at would be a settling for lower stakes than those of the incarnation. It is not that the priest is the only person worthy enough – no one is worthy. Only a certain setting-aside by the whole community is worthy, hand in hand with the particular kind of life lived as a result.

Setting aside for life

A priest may understand such a setting-aside as a self-offering (which it will hopefully be), but there are pitfalls in that, for from it can come self-motivation and self-dramatization. The perfect sacrifice looks away from self towards the other, largely unaware that there is any sacrifice. While it is good to appeal to a sense of sacrifice when seeking vocations, and while the truth about sacrifice has to undergird the priesthood, it isn't possible in practice to speak quite like that. Sacrifice is no monopoly of the clergy. The core of the matter is not in self-giving, but in the call from God to act out that drastic-ness which gives the gospel its edge.

Clergy on the whole are not ordained as lambs to the slaughter – it is usually a happy experience. The point is not in any personal sense of sacrifice, but is found in the clear, straight generosity required that 'you will apply yourselves wholly to this one thing, and draw all your cares and studies this way' (Book of Common Prayer, 'Form and manner of ordaining priests').

Keeping the geyser going

There are some aspects of Christian life that we see as 'deeply personal'. The focal nature of priesthood means that the personal becomes public and objective too. No priest can have perfect faith, cast-iron and watertight – that would be so removed from daily life that we could suspect it of self-deception and illusion. Any fragility in the priest's own faith and life will ring true with people, and neither popular expectation nor official ecclesiastical requirement can expect anything else. One rightly public expectation is that what needs to be done will get done – prayer public and private, public worship and administration of the word and sacraments, done with care, pastoral diligence and competence, even when the priest doesn't feel like it. In this sense the priest is the quorum, the ultimate reduction of the faithfulness of the Church, the place where the buck stops, the one place in the life of the local church where its life will not stop, even if it should stop everywhere else. The priest is the pilot light in the parish's geyser. Sometimes the geyser is in operation, sometimes it isn't, but the pilot light never goes out, and the geyser is viable. Even though there may be many Christians in the parish of exemplary faith whose lives are a shining beacon, there is still the practical need for one commissioned and set aside to ensure the framework within which such things can live.

At its simplest it is practical. The worldwide people of God are supported by a network of plumbing, which brings certain practical necessities to each local community. Just as the set liturgy and laws cascade down through the network, so also does the provision of commissioned persons. The Twelve must certainly have had something about them for Jesus to choose them, but to judge from their behaviour both before and after his death, he could have chosen better, had he worked harder at it. The main thing in the end was that they were there and that they set about the required task. Mercifully, there was, and is, more than just guaranteed minimum service in the Church's shepherds, but it can still be said that, even if in a time of darkness all the lights go out, the priest's will not. The Scriptures will be delved, the prayers said, and the sacraments administered, and for that, grace is given whenever it is asked.

So the priest, taken up totally by God for a purpose; the priest, a whole offering of a human life, sustains the response to that call through thick and thin, fed by prayer and study, by steeping in the scriptures, by closeness to people and closeness to the sacraments, and by an in-touch-ness with the wider Church that cannot be assumed in other Christian believers, even if it is hoped for. Broken open by suffering and trials, sometimes almost overwhelmed by a sense of personal frailty, yet is the priest God's person in that place for the sake of the people.

A 'life'

How can all the bits of such a bitty life be held together? The nuts and bolts of priesthood include: leading worship, daily office and prayer, intercession, visiting and general pastoral work, counsel, administration, the priest's family, recreation, tensions, confrontations, worries, maintenance of church, house and garden, the necessities of eating, cleaning, shopping, finance, and so on. Piling on top of everything else come, in Macmillan's famous phrase, 'Events, dear boy, events'. It can be frustrating to have to do the shopping when so many important things clamour for attention, maddening to make time to listen to an inane conversation when more pressing things need to be done, and there are many 'if only's' about jobs that ought to have been done by others, freeing the priest for the proper task. Tensions and clamouring demands pull in all directions, many things are left half done, other undone tasks sow seeds of guilt and disappointment. You are pulled in every direction, and nothing gets the attention or the time it deserves.

If, however, the main task is seen to be priestly – the task of offering it all up, accepting all God sends – then let it all come, let it all flow over me and through me, and the whole, absolutely the whole lot, is seen as one priestly offering. Then the picture changes. Then you see that you are living not in fragments, but a whole life. All the bits have their place: shopping, cleaning the car, burying the dead, counselling the troubled, day off at the seaside, sewing on buttons, a night out at the pictures, all an integrated whole. Most of it will have ragged edges, but there is no need to feel greatly guilt or disappointed, or frustrated. *The main work is the living of it as an integrated whole, the total being-there and living-it-out of the priest in community.* This is not a romantic subterfuge to smooth over cracks: it is more a matter of having our eyes opened to life as it really is. The whole of our life is permeated with the divine Mystery, and is a priestly celebration of the liturgy. This then helps us have the liberty to distribute the parts in a more balanced way. Most of it will have an unfinished air about it, but that is how it will be. Some of it, furthermore, will have to go. The priest needs the courage to ditch some things that are worthy and important. The *aim* will be not to get as much done as possible in the 'worthy' areas, while being pinpricked by personal and household *mundane* needs getting in the way, but to see it all as a whole life, an all-embracing way of being. If this way of living takes up its place in me, then when I am having to do the shopping there is no need to be anxious that I ought to be visiting; when doing administration and deskwork, no fear this is getting in the way of the real work: it is a whole life, offered up as it is, for what it is, a sweet-smelling sacrifice, with its own unity located in God.

The Church from below and the Church from above

Without the Church, the priest or any ordained minister is nothing. In this service and calling, the sense of who you are, and the idea of it having sense, come ultimately from two directions. On the one hand, there is the body of Christ as a family of human beings trying with the help of

God to find their way. On the other, like an overarching vault, there is the givenness of the sovereignty of God, creating the Church and calling it into life. That givenness incarnates itself in the objective practices of the calling. To get on with the daily prayers and the worship, the study and the hurly-burly, the breaking of bread and the life of the community, whatever we might be inclined to feel at the time, is to find repose in that overarching givenness. Great is the Mystery of our faith, incarnate in these concrete things; Jesus Christ holding out to us this sense of repose, the gift of faith.

The things we have examined in this book all come down to one focal point, where the Christian community, conscious of its communion with the great Church on earth and in heaven, looks on the ministry exercised by its priest and says, 'This is a priesthood which is both yours and ours.'

Notes

1 The Priest and the Mystery

1 Garrison Keillor, *Lake Wobegon Days* (London: Faber, 1986), p. 141.

2 *Lumen Gentium*, Dogmatic Constitution on the Church, 21 November 1964, in *Vatican Council II: The Conciliar and Post Conciliar Documents*, revised edition, edited by Austin Flannery OP (Dublin: Dominican Publications, 1992), pp. 350–426.

3 Denis E. Hurley OMI, 'Bishops, presbyterate and the training of priests', in *Modern Catholicism: Vatican II and After*, edited by Adrian Hastings (London: SPCK, 1991), pp. 141–50 (p. 141). A discussion of the relevant Vatican II documents.

4 Brian O'Sullivan, 'The spirituality of the diocesan priest', *Priests and People*, vol. 11, no. 3 (March 1997), pp. 105–7 (pp. 105–6).

5 J. D. Crichton, *Lights in the Darkness: Forerunners of the Liturgical Movement* (Dublin: Columba Press, 1996).

6 Thomas Merton, *No Man is an Island* (London: Burns & Oates, 1955), p. 125.

7 Austin Farrer, 'Walking sacraments' [1968], in *A Celebration of Faith: Communications, mostly to Students* (London: Hodder & Stoughton, 1970), p. 109.

8 For a discussion of this, with statistics and full consideration of its implications, see *Europe without Priests?*, edited by Jan Kerkhofs SJ (London: SCM, 1995).

9 Michael Richards, *A People of Priests: The Ministry of the Catholic Church* (London: DLT, 1995), p. 3.

10 Alwyn Marriage, *The People of God: A Royal Priesthood* (London: DLT, 1995), p. 2.

11 Alberto Manguel, 'How those plastic stones speak: the renewed struggle between the codex and the scroll', *Times Literary Supplement*, 4 July 1997, pp. 8–9), p. 8.

12 Peter Schmidt, 'Ministries in the New Testament and the early Church', in *Europe without Priests?*, ed. Kerkhofs, pp. 41–88 (p. 61).

13 Henri de Lubac SJ, *Christian Faith: The Structure of the Apostles' Creed* (London: Geoffrey Chapman, 1986), p. 52, quoting St Bernard, *De consideratione*, 5, 6. The Proverbs reference is to the Vulgate text of Prov. 25.27: *sic qui scrutator est majestatis opprimetur a gloria*.

14 Karl Rahner SJ, 'Mystery', in *Encyclopedia of Theology: The Concise Sacramentum Mundi*, edited by K. Rahner (London: Burns & Oates, 1975), pp. 1000–4 (p. 1001).

15 Rahner, 'Mystery', p. 1001.

16 Rudolf Otto, *The Idea of the Holy* (London: OUP, 1923), p. 31.

17 Gustave Martelet SJ, *The Risen Christ and the Eucharistic World*, trans. T. Corbishley SJ (London: Collins, 1976), p. 104. For more detail on Casel's mystery theology, its context, and its impact on eucharistic and liturgical theology and the idea of 'presence', see Martelet, *The Risen Christ*, pp. 101ff. and more recently

George Guiver CR, *Pursuing the Mystery: Worship and Daily Life as Presences of God* (London: SPCK, 1996), ch. 5. For the impact of Casel's thought on Anglican liturgical life, see also Christopher Irvine, *Worship, Church and Society: An Exposition of the Work of Arthur Gabriel Hebert* (Norwich: Canterbury Press, 1993), pp. 103–5.

18 *Sacrosanctam Concilium*, The Constitution on the Sacred Liturgy, 4 December 1963, in *Vatican Council II Documents*, ed. Flannery, pp. 1–36 (section 7, pp. 4–5).

19 St Ambrose, *On the Mysteries (De mysteriis)*, iii, 15.

20 Odo Casel OSB, *The Mystery of Christian Worship*, English edition (London: DLT, 1962), p. 25.

21 Casel, *Mystery*, p. 25.

22 See also Chapter 10.

23 Edward King, letter to an ordinand, August 1873, in *Spiritual Letters* (London: Mowbray, 1910), p. 37.

24 King, to the same on his ordination to the priesthood, May 1874, *Spiritual Letters*, pp. 38–9.

25 Richard Meux Benson SSJE, to a mission priest newly ordained, 1888, in *Spiritual Letters*, edited by W. H. Longridge SSJE (London: Mowbray, 1924), pp. 148–9.

26 Robin Greenwood, *Transforming Priesthood: A New Theology of Mission and Ministry* (London: SPCK, 1994).

27 For a discussion of Rahner's thought in this area see Michael Skelley SJ, *The Liturgy of the World: Karl Rahner's Theology of Worship* (Collegeville: Pueblo, 1991).

28 Graham Greene, *The Honorary Consul* (London: Penguin, 1974), p. 109.

29 Graham Greene, *The Lawless Roads* (London: Heinemann, 1939); *The Power and the Glory* (London: Heinemann, 1940). Available in many Penguin paperback editions.

30 The photograph of Padre Pro is in Norman Sherry, *The Life of Graham Greene: Volume One 1904–1939* (London: Jonathan Cape, 1989), plate 75 between pp. 714–15.

31 See Chapter 7.

32 St Ambrose, *On the Mysteries*, ii, 6.

33 For further exploration of this see Chapter 10.

34 Thomas Brett, Sermon on the Priesthood (1712), quoted in Martin Thornton, 'The Anglican tradition of priesthood', in his *Essays in Pastoral Reconstruction* (London: SPCK, 1960), pp. 35–47 (pp. 38–9).

35 Austin Farrer, sermon at an ordination, May 1961, published in *Theology*, xciv (1991), pp. 166–7 (p. 166).

36 Thornton, 'Anglican tradition of priesthood', p. 43.

37 For a more detailed discussion of social roles and the controversial issue of sexuality in priesthood, see Chapter 8.

38 Thornton, 'Anglican tradition of priesthood', p. 43.

39 George Herbert, *A Priest to the Temple, or The Country Parson, His Character, and Rule of Holy Life* (1652), ch. 17.

40 Farrer, ordination sermon, 1961, p. 167.

41 Thomas Merton, *The Sign of Jonas* (London: Hollis & Carter, 1953), pp. 177–8.

2 Screen Idol

1 Church of England, *Lent, Holy Week and Easter* (CHP, CUP, SPCK, 1984), p. 90.

2 Leo the Great, *Sermon 4*, in *The Divine Office* (London: Collins, 1974), vol. III, p. 387.

3 J. H. Newman, *Parochial and Plain Sermons (1836-8)*, vol. III, sermon 19, pp. 271ff. (cf. www.newmanreader.org).

3 The Priest in the Media Age

1 For example, Len Masterman, *Teaching the Media* (London: Comedia, 1985), *passim*.

2 Neil Simpson, in *Religion and the Media*, edited by Chris Arthur (Cardiff: University of Wales Press, 1993), p. 106.

3 Albeit with the help of ammonia in his holy water bottle to squirt into the Zombie-master's eyes – Anthony Burgess, *Earthly Powers* (Penguin edition, 1981), pp. 271ff.

4 Charles Pickstone, *For Fear of the Angels: How Sex Has Usurped Religion* (London: Hodder, 1996), p. 124f.

5 Simon Schama, *Landscape and Memory* (London: HarperCollins, 1995). See, for example, ch. 4 *passim*.

6 Schama, *Landscape*, p. 186.

7 Thomas Hardy, 'Convergence of the Twain', lines on the loss of the *Titanic*.

8 Arthur, *Religion*, p. 108.

9 Arthur, *Religion*, p. 14.

10 Arthur, *Religion*, p. 16.

11 Neil Simpson in Arthur, *Religion*, p. 105.

12 It is an interesting question as to whether the priest creates sacred space or vice versa – whether a sacred space permits the priest to be a priest.

13 R. S. Thomas, *Frequencies* (London: Macmillan, 1978), p. 45.

14 *[le] prince des nuées/Qui hante la tempête et se rit de l'archer*.

15 *Ses ailes de géant/l'empêchent de marcher*, Baudelaire, *Les Fleurs du Mal*, Florenne edition; Paris: Livre de Poche, 1972, p. 179f.

16 David A. Hart, *Linking Up: Christianity and Sexuality* (London: Arthur James, 1997), p. 4.

17 The story is well told by Andy McSmith in his *Faces of Labour* (London: Verso, 1996), p. 87.

18 This scene does not occur in Miller's original play: it is entirely Hollywood.

19 'Certain farms which had belonged to the victims were left to ruin, and for more than a century no one would buy them or live on them. To all intents and purposes, the power of theocracy in Massachusetts was broken.' Arthur Miller, *The Crucible* (Harmondsworth: Penguin, 1972), p. 127.

20 Mary Charles Murray, 'Predicazione della parola e immagine' in *Christianesimo nella Storia* (Bologna University Press, 1993), pp. 481–503.

21 Dorothee Sölle, quoted by Arthur, *Religion*, p. 17.

22 Dennis Potter's phrase in an interview on BBC1, 25 August 1987, following a screening of his *Brimstone and Treacle*.

23 A phrase of Pier Paolo Pasolini quoted by Dorothee Sölle in her article in Arthur, *Religion*, p. 226.

24 Neil Postman, *Amusing Ourselves to Death* (London: Heinemann, 1986), p. 87.

25 *Daily Mail*, 12 July 1997, p. 14, in the context of Fr Alex Coker, ousted from his post by the Bishop of Croydon in May 1994.

26 Sölle in Arthur, *Religion*, p. 233.

4 A Word from One of the *Laos*

1 F. Dostoyevsky, *The Brothers Karamazov* (London: Penguin, 1993).

2 Edmund Flood, *The Laity Today and Tomorrow*.

3 Vincent J. Donovan, *Christianity Rediscovered: An Epistle from the Masai* (London: SCM, 1982), pp. 158–9.

4 Kenneth Leech, *The Sky is Red: Discerning the Signs of the Times* (London: DLT, 1970), pp. 120–4.

5 Tim Gorringe, *Alan Ecclestone: Priest as Revolutionary: A Biography* (Sheffield: Cirns Publications, 1994), p. 104.

6 Gorringe, *Alan Ecclestone*, p. 104.

7 Gorringe, *Alan Ecclestone*, p. 98.

5 Simple Gifts

1 Eighteenth-century Shaker song, Hymn 554 in *The Hymnal 1982* (New York: Church Hymnal Corporation).

2 Migne, *Patrologia Graeca* (Paris, 1860), vol. 91, columns 4–53ff.

6 Priest and Victim

1 R. Girard, *Things Hidden Since the Foundation of the World* (Stanford University Press, 1993).

2 Benedicta Ward SLG, *Sayings of the Desert Fathers* (Cistercian Publications, 1975) p. 134.

3 Ward, *Sayings*, p. 117.

4 Anne Wroe, 'Don't blame me, I'm a victim', *Tablet*, 8 November 1997, p. 1433

5 See: George Guiver CR, *Pursuing the Mystery* (London: SPCK, 1996).

8 The Priest, Sex and Society

1 Quotes from John Collins, *Are All Christians Ministers?* (Australia: Dwyer, 1992), pp. 3–4.

2 John Collins, *Diakonia* (OUP, 1990).

3 K. Mason, *Priesthood and Society* (Norwich: Canterbury Press, 1992).

4 Alasdair MacIntyre, *After Virtue* (Duckworth, 1981).

5 Charles Taylor, *Sources of the Self: The Making of the Modern Identity* (CUP, 1989).

6 M. Foucault, *History of Sexuality* (London: Penguin, 1998).

7 *Rule of St Benedict*, 53.

8 R. Gill, *Moral Communities* (University of Exeter Press, 1992).

9 Detachment in Priesthood and Community

1 Graham Greene, *The Heart of the Matter* (London: Penguin, 1962), p. 272.

2 Peter France, *Hermits: The Insights of Solitude* (London: Pimlico, 1997), pp. xi–xii.

3 Perran Gay, 'Seeing life whole: an integrative approach to the Christian tradition', in *New Soundings: Essays on Developing Tradition*, edited by S. Platten, G. James and A. Chandler (London: DLT, 1997), pp. 58–75 (p. 73).

4 Richard Barrett, 'The priest as artist', *New Blackfriars* (February 1998), pp. 84–96 (p. 88).

5 This was an incident that occurred in the author's ministry in a small market town.

6 Ps. 107.25–30 in the version contained in *Celebrating Common Prayer* (Mowbray, 1992).

7 Henri J. M. Nouwen, *Intimacy: Pastoral Psychological Essays* (Notre Dame, 1968), p. 119.

8 'For the glory of God is a living man; and the life of man is the vision of God', Irenaeus, *Adversus Haereses*, IV.xx.6, in *The Early Christian Fathers*, edited by H. Bettenson (Oxford, 1956), pp. 75–6.

9 Barrett, 'The priest as artist', p. 88.

Index

absolution, 80
Ahwahneechee Indians, 40
Ambrose, St, 8, 12, 18, 19
Anglican Church
    shortage of ministers, 6–7
Antony of Egypt, St, 130
apostolic mission, 9
Aquinas, Thomas, 99
Augustine, St, 8, 46

baptism
    identity, 67
    and ordination, 4–5
    and priesthood of Christ, 6, 13
Baptism, Eucharist and Ministry,
    103
Barrett, R., 119 (quoted)
Baudelaire, Charles, 43
Beckett, Wendy, 45
Benedict, St, 97, 108
Benson, Richard Meux, 14
Bernard, St, 9
Binyon, Laurence, 41
Bonhoeffer, Dietrich, 67
Book of Common Prayer, 135
Brett, Thomas, 19
Bunyan, John, 66
Burgess, Anthony, 38

Carter, Sydney, 63
Casel, Odo, 11, 13, 79
Catholic Crusade, 58

Chaplin, Charlie, 26
Chrysostom, John, 133
clerical dress, 15–18
College of the Resurrection, 25, 132
Collins, John, 104
community
    Christian, 112–13
    local, 116–17
compassion, 78
confirmation, 13
conversion, 67
Copland, Aaron, 63
Cover, Jean, 42
Crichton, J. D., 6
crisis in ministry, 6–8

Dahl, Roald, 10
Day, Doris, 26
Day-Lewis, Daniel, 45
death, 41
de Lubac, Henri, 9
Diaconal Association of the Church
    of England, 52–3
diaconate, 52–3
Diana, Princess, 41
Dickinson, Emily, 63
Director, 44
discretio, 108–9, 131–2
Donne, John, 66
Donovan, Vincent, 54–5
Dostoyevsky, F., 51 (quoted)

Eappen, Matthew, 77
Ecclestone, Alan, 57
Erasmus, 131
Eucharist, 13, 51, 53, 57, 80–1, 135
    lay presidency, 7
    unity in diversity, 59
Europe without Priests?, 9, 14

faith, 135-6
Federation of the Evangelical
    Churches, 103
First World War, 40–1
Farrer, Austin, 6, 20, 22
Flood, E., 53
Ford, Harrison, 26
For Fear of Angels, 38
Foucault, Michel, 107
France, Peter, 118–19
freedom, 65–6
French, Dawn, 36
Frere, Walter, 132
fundamentalism, 44–5

'getting alongside', 115–16
Gill, Robin, 112
Girard, René, 75, 76, 79
Gorringe, Tim, 57
Grantham, Leslie, 37
Greene, Graham, 15, 16–17, 111,
    117
Greenwood, Robin, 14

Hare, David, 38
Harries, Richard, 58
Henderson, Don, 37
Herbert, George, 21, 97
hermit tradition, 118–21
Holy Spirit, 13–14, 117
humanity
    of Christ, 18–19
    of priests, 19–23
Hurley, D. E., 4 (quoted)

Independent, 44
integrity, 104–6
interdependence, 51
Issues in Human Sexuality, 58

Jesus Christ
    humanity of, 18–19, 79–80
    ministry, 68–71
    model, 78–9
    nature of presence, 11–13,
        108–9, 115–16
    paschal mystery, 15, 17
    as priest, 29
John XXIII, Pope, 5, 38

Keillor, Garrison, 3, 20
Kellner, Peter, 44
King, Edward, 14
Kinnock, Neil, 44

Labour Party, 44
laity, 51–9
    individual needs, 56–7
    interdependence with
        priesthood, 51, 58
    mutual respect, 51–2
    pastoral work, 55
    prayer, 55–6
    training, 55
    unity in diversity, 58–9
Lambeth Conference (1998), 108
Lawrence, St, 52
leadership, 116, 134
Leech, Kenneth, 56
Leo the Great, Pope, 30
Lewisham People's Day, 33
Liturgical Movement, 5–6

MacIntyre, Alasdair, 105, 110
Macmillan, Harold, 137
Marc, Franz, 41

marriage, 85–99
  covenant, 87
  holy ideal, 110
  sacramental function, 86
Marriage, Alwyn, 7
Mar Thoma Church, 98
Masai, 54
Mason, Kenneth, 104
Maximus, St, 68
media
  portrayals, 34–9, 102, 104, 106
  use of, 43–6
Merton, Thomas, 6, 22
Methodist Covenant Prayer, 65
Mexico, 16–17
Miller, Arthur, 45–6
monastic priesthood, 63–71
monastic vows, 64–5
Morris, Michael, 45
Murdoch, Iris, 110
Murray, Mary Charles, 46
mutual respect, 51–2
mystery, 3–23, 79–80
  Christ's nature, 18–19
  language of, 10–11
  in liturgy, 13
  of marriage, 85–7
  presence of Christ, 11–13
  and sacrament, 11
  and Scripture, 8–10

Newman, J. H., 31 (quoted)
Nietzsche, Friedrich, 33, 40
Nimmo, Derek, 36
Nouwen, Henri, 123

ordination service, 27
O'Sullivan, B., 5 (quoted)
Otto, Rudolf, 10
Owen, Wilfred, 41

parish meeting, 57–8
partnership, 134–5
paschal mystery, 15, 17
Paul VI, Pope, 5
performance, 33–4
Pius X, Pope, 52
poetry, 41, 43
'Popular Religion on TV', 36
Postman, Neil, 47
prayer life, 5, 55–6, 89, 97–8,
  121–2, 123–4
Priest, 37, 102, 106
priesthood
  Christological aspect, 18
  and marriage, 90–9, 110
  models, 102–4
  shared by all, 30–1
  sign value, 12, 81, 89
  way of being, 87–90
priests
  as focus of parish, 127–38
  as outsiders, 132–3
  as prophets, 47–8, 96–8
  total commitment, 129–32
Pro, Miguel, 17
psalms, 80

Rahner, K., 10 (quoted), 15
reconciliation, 80
relaxation, 130–2
representatives of Christ, 27–30
rhetoric, 46–7
Richards, Michael, 7
Ricoeur, Paul, 38
Roman Catholic Church, 4, 5, 37
  shortage of priests, 6, 55, 104
Royle, Roger, 34

sacramental theology, 11
sacred space, 39–43

Sandham Memorial Chapel, 41
Sawalha, Julia, 36
Schama, Simon, 39, 40
Schleifer, S. A., 42
Scripture, 8–10
Sea of Faith, 129
Second Vatican Council, 4, 5
    Lumen Gentium, 4
    Sacrosanctum Concilium, 12
        (quoted)
self-offering, 135, 137
sexuality, 38, 101–13
sexual morality, 107–8, 111–13
Sisters of the Love of God, 63
Society of St John the Evangelist,
    14
Sölle, Dorothee, 48
Spencer, Stanley, 41
spirituality, 123–4
    see also prayer life
Stewart, James, 27
stole, symbolism of, 28–29

Tablet, 58
Taylor, Charles, 105
theology of priesthood
    need for, 4, 7–8
Thomas, R. S., 43
Thornton, Martin, 20, 21
tradition, 109–10
training of laity, 55

unity in diversity, 58–9
Urwin, Lindsay, 30

Valentino, Rudolph, 25
Vicar of Dibley, 36–7
victims, 73–8, 81–2
vocation, 64, 102–4

Wesley, John, 89
women
    diaconate, 52
    ordination of, 7

Yosemite National Park, 39–40